Eco Endeavors: A Handbook of Off-Grid Projects

Crafting a Greener, Smarter, and Independent Lifestyle

Mason Campbell

Table of Contents

INTRODUCTION

Welcome to "Eco Endeavors: A Handbook of Off-Grid Projects - Crafting a Greener, Smarter, and Independent Lifestyle." In a world marked by rapid urbanization, heightened environmental awareness, and an increasing desire for self-sufficiency, off-grid living has emerged as a beacon of sustainable, resilient, and mindful existence. This handbook is your comprehensive guide to embracing the off-grid lifestyle, offering a wealth of knowledge, practical insights, and innovative projects that empower you to create a greener, more intelligent, and more independent life.

The journey into off-grid living begins with a fundamental shift in mindset and a commitment to reducing reliance on conventional resources. In the opening chapters, we explore the essence of off-grid living, discussing its benefits, challenges, and the transformative impact it can have on your life. From cultivating a deeper connection with nature to gaining unparalleled self-sufficiency, each aspect is dissected to provide a holistic understanding of living off the grid.

Arming you with the skills necessary for off-grid living, we delve into survival essentials, DIY repairs, and resourceful cooking techniques. These fundamental skills form the backbone of your journey toward self-sufficiency, ensuring that you can adapt to challenges and thrive in your new lifestyle.

Chapters dedicated to energy solutions and water management equip you with the knowledge to harness the power of renewable resources. Discover the intricacies of installing solar power systems, wind turbines, and effective rainwater harvesting techniques. Learn how to not only conserve but thrive with minimal environmental impact.

As you embark on this transformative journey through "Eco Endeavors," you will find a roadmap to construct a more sustainable, eco-friendly, and fulfilling lifestyle. Join us as we navigate the exciting realm of off-grid projects, fostering a community of individuals dedicated to crafting a future that is not just sustainable but genuinely regenerative.

CHAPTER I

The Off-Grid Lifestyle

Understanding Off-Grid Living

In a world dominated by modern conveniences, off-grid living is a bold departure from conventional lifestyles. It represents a commitment to self-sufficiency, sustainability, and a deep connection with the natural environment. Off-grid living entails relying on decentralized and renewable resources to meet one's daily needs, emancipating individuals from the grid of mainstream utilities and fostering a sense of autonomy. This lifestyle shift involves a profound understanding of the benefits and challenges inherent in disconnecting from traditional power sources, water supplies, and urban infrastructure.

Embarking on the journey of off-grid living requires a paradigm shift—reevaluating the relationship between individuals and their environment. The allure lies in pursuing environmental consciousness and the desire for a more spartan, more intentional existence. One of the primary advantages of off-grid living is the reduced ecological footprint. By generating energy through sustainable means such as solar panels or wind turbines, individuals minimize their reliance on fossil fuels and contribute to mitigating climate change. Generating power locally, often on-site, reduces transmission losses associated with centralized power grids, making off-grid living an environmentally responsible choice.

However, the decision to embrace an off-grid lifestyle is challenging. The initial transition involves a departure from the familiar comforts of mainstream living, requiring a comprehensive understanding of the trade-offs involved. The absence of a direct connection to municipal utilities means individuals must assume responsibility for their energy production, water supply, and waste management. This demands a level of self-sufficiency that may be unfamiliar to those accustomed to the convenience of flipping a switch for electricity or turning a tap for water.

One of the defining features of off-grid living is the need to adopt a mindset that prioritizes resourcefulness and adaptability. This lifestyle encourages individuals to become more attuned to the rhythms of nature, adapting daily routines to harness the power of the sun, wind, and other natural elements. The off-grid dweller becomes intimately acquainted with the cycles of renewable resources, learning to optimize energy consumption during peak production times and adjust activities accordingly. This attunement to nature fosters a more profound connection with the environment and serves as a practical guide for sustainable living.

In addition to environmental considerations, off-grid living offers a unique opportunity for individuals to reassess their consumption patterns and embrace a more intentional lifestyle. The reduction of reliance on external resources prompts a reevaluation of what is essential, leading to a minimalist approach to material possessions. Off-grid living encourages a shift from consumerism to sustainability, focusing on quality over quantity and a commitment to repurposing and recycling.

The benefits of off-grid living extend beyond personal well-being and environmental stewardship. The lifestyle promotes independence and resilience in the face of external challenges. Off-grid dwellers develop practical skills, from basic survival techniques to DIY repairs and maintenance. This newfound self-sufficiency enhances one's ability to navigate the intricacies of off-grid living and fosters a sense of empowerment and confidence.

Yet, the challenges of off-grid living are not to be underestimated. The initial setup costs for off-grid infrastructure can be substantial, requiring a significant investment in renewable energy systems, water management solutions, and sustainable shelter. Furthermore, the learning curve associated with acquiring the skills necessary for self-sufficiency may be steep for those accustomed to the convenience of urban living. The potential for isolation, especially in remote off-grid locations, poses a psychological challenge that individuals must navigate.

The decision to embrace off-grid living is inherently tied to a desire for a closer connection with nature. For many, the draw lies in escaping the hustle and bustle of urban life, immersing themselves in the tranquility of natural surroundings. Off-grid dwellers often choose locations characterized by pristine landscapes, allowing them to live harmoniously with the environment. Whether nestled in a dense forest, perched on a mountainside, or overlooking a serene valley, off-grid homes become sanctuaries that celebrate the beauty of the natural world.

In conclusion, understanding off-grid living is a nuanced exploration of the delicate balance between environmental stewardship, self-sufficiency, and intentional living. It involves a conscious decision to break free from the constraints of mainstream infrastructure and embrace a lifestyle that prioritizes harmony with nature. The journey towards off-grid living is not without its challenges, but the rewards—both for the individual and the planet—are profound. As we delve into the intricacies of this lifestyle, we uncover a tapestry of sustainability, resilience, and the timeless connection between humans and the Earth.

Benefits and Challenges

The decision to embrace an off-grid lifestyle is a profound choice with many benefits and challenges. At its essence, the allure of off-grid living lies in the pursuit of sustainability, self-sufficiency, and a closer connection with nature. As individuals navigate the path to disconnect from traditional power sources, water supplies, and urban infrastructure, they embark on a journey marked by rewards and complexities.

One of the primary benefits of off-grid living is the reduced environmental impact. By generating energy through renewable sources such as solar panels, wind turbines, or hydropower, off-grid dwellers significantly decrease their reliance on fossil fuels. This shift contributes to climate change mitigation, as the decentralized nature of off-grid energy production minimizes transmission losses associated with centralized power grids. Off-grid living becomes a tangible expression of environmental consciousness, offering a lifestyle that aligns with sustainability principles.

Moreover, reducing reliance on municipal utilities translates into a smaller ecological footprint. Off-grid dwellers often implement water conservation measures, harness rainwater for domestic use, and adopt composting toilets to manage waste. These practices not only contribute to the preservation of natural resources but also serve as examples of eco-friendly living for a broader audience. Off-grid living catalyzes a more sustainable and responsible relationship with the environment.

In addition to environmental benefits, off-grid living fosters a sense of self-sufficiency and resilience. By becoming less dependent on external sources for energy, water, and food, individuals acquire practical skills that enhance their ability to navigate challenges. From basic survival techniques to do-it-yourself repairs and maintenance, off-grid dwellers develop resourcefulness beyond their immediate environment. This newfound independence empowers individuals to face uncertainties confidently, reinforcing that self-sufficiency is not merely a lifestyle choice but a mindset that can be applied to various aspects of life.

However, the benefits of off-grid living are accompanied by a unique set of challenges that individuals must navigate. One of the foremost challenges is the initial investment required for off-grid infrastructure. Setting up solar power systems, wind turbines, water management solutions, and sustainable shelters demands a significant financial commitment. While the long-term savings on utility bills may offset these costs, the upfront investment can be a barrier for those considering the transition to off- grid living.

The learning curve associated with acquiring the skills necessary for self-sufficiency is another challenge that off-grid dwellers must confront. Individuals accustomed to the conveniences of urban living may grapple with the intricacies of energy production, water purification, and waste management. The transition from simply consuming resources to actively producing and managing them requires a mindset shift and a commitment to ongoing learning. This learning curve can be steep and time-consuming, demanding patience and perseverance from those embarking on the off-grid journey.

Moreover, the potential for isolation poses a psychological challenge for off-grid dwellers, particularly those residing in remote locations. The disconnect from urban amenities and the sparse population density can lead to feelings of loneliness and social isolation. Building a sense of community becomes crucial in mitigating this challenge, and off-grid dwellers often find creative ways to connect with like-minded individuals, whether through online forums, community events, or shared resources. Overcoming the isolation challenge requires a proactive approach to fostering connections and building a supportive network.

Another aspect of off-grid living that individuals must contend with is careful resource management. Without municipal services, off-grid dwellers must optimize their energy consumption, water usage, and waste generation. This requires a heightened awareness of natural cycles, weather patterns, and the limitations of local resources. While resource management is integral to sustainable living, it can pose a daily challenge that demands diligence and adaptability.

Yet, within the challenges of off-grid living lies an opportunity for personal growth and a deepened connection with the environment. Overcoming the hurdles of financial investment, skill acquisition, and potential isolation fosters resilience and adaptability. The challenges become stepping stones toward a more intentional and fulfilling lifestyle, reinforcing that the benefits of off-grid living extend beyond environmental considerations.

In conclusion, the benefits and challenges of off-grid living form a delicate balance that individuals must navigate as they embrace a lifestyle centered on sustainability and self-sufficiency. The rewards of reduced environmental impact, enhanced self-sufficiency, and a closer connection with nature underscore the transformative potential of off-grid living. Simultaneously, initial investment, skill acquisition, isolation, and resource management challenges highlight the commitment and resilience required for this lifestyle. As individuals weigh the pros and cons, they embark on a journey that transcends the boundaries of conventional living, offering a glimpse into a future where intentional, eco-conscious choices shape a more harmonious relationship between humanity and the planet.

Making the Decision to Go Off-Grid

The decision to embark on the off-grid lifestyle is a transformative journey that necessitates careful consideration, introspection, and a deep understanding of one's values and priorities. It represents a departure from the conventional trajectory of urban living, where centralized utilities, modern conveniences, and a bustling community dictate the rhythm of daily life. Going off-grid is a decision to redefine the relationship with the environment and prioritize self-sufficiency, sustainability, and a connection with nature.

At the core of the decision to go off-grid lies a fundamental question: what drives the desire for a lifestyle that diverges from the norm? For many, the motivation is rooted in a longing for a more intentional and meaningful existence. Off-grid living offers a departure from the relentless pace of urban life, inviting individuals to embrace a slower, more deliberate way of living. The allure of waking up to the sounds of nature, breathing in fresh, unpolluted air, and living in harmony with the land becomes a compelling force that prompts a reevaluation of priorities.

Environmental consciousness plays a pivotal role in the decision to go off-grid. As climate change and ecological degradation become increasingly urgent global concerns, individuals seeking a more sustainable lifestyle find solace in the off-grid ethos. The desire to reduce one's ecological footprint, minimize reliance on non-renewable resources, and actively contribute to environmental preservation becomes a driving force in the decision-making process. Off-grid living represents a personal commitment to living in harmony with the Earth, a tangible manifestation of the belief that sustainable choices on an individual level can collectively make a significant impact.

Financial considerations also factor prominently into the decision to go off-grid. While the upfront costs of setting up off-grid infrastructure can be substantial, the long-term savings on utility bills and the potential for a more frugal lifestyle can be compelling incentives. Individuals seeking financial independence, freedom from monthly bills, and a break from the consumerist cycle find a path toward economic autonomy in off-grid living. The prospect of investing in renewable energy systems, water harvesting, and sustainable shelter becomes not just an expense but an investment in a future characterized by reduced financial stress and increased self-reliance.

Self-sufficiency, a cornerstone of off-grid living, emerges as a powerful motivator in decision-making. The desire to produce energy, grow food, and manage resources independently reflects a yearning for autonomy. Off-grid living transforms individuals from passive consumers of services to active contributors to their well-being, requiring a shift in mindset from dependence on external systems to the empowerment of self-sufficiency. This transition aligns with a more profound philosophical exploration of what it means to live a fulfilling and purposeful life.

Yet, the decision to go off-grid has its complexities and challenges. The romanticized vision of a simpler life amidst nature must contend with the practicalities of setting up and maintaining off-grid infrastructure. The initial investment in solar panels, wind turbines, water management systems, and sustainable housing can be a significant barrier for many. The financial commitment requires a thoughtful assessment of short-term sacrifices against the long-term benefits, prompting individuals to weigh the immediate costs against the future rewards of a sustainable and self-sufficient lifestyle.

Moreover, going off-grid demands a willingness to embrace a steep learning curve. Off-grid living requires a diverse skill set, from understanding renewable energy systems to mastering water purification techniques and cultivating food sustainably. Individuals accustomed to the conveniences of urban living may find themselves challenged by the need to adapt to a more hands-on and resourceful approach. The commitment to ongoing learning becomes integral to the off-grid journey, requiring individuals to become consumers and active participants in managing their daily needs.

Social considerations also play a role in the decision-making process. The potential for isolation, especially in remote off-grid locations, raises questions about the impact on personal relationships and the need for a supportive community. Individuals contemplating the shift to off-grid living must weigh the desire for solitude and tranquility against the human need for connection and companionship. Building a community of like-minded individuals becomes an essential aspect of the decision to go off-grid, providing both practical support and a sense of belonging.

In essence, deciding to go off-grid is a multifaceted process that involves aligning personal values with practical considerations. It explores what truly matters— environmental stewardship, financial autonomy, or a quest for a more intentional and meaningful existence. The decision reflects a commitment to break away from the conventional narrative of modern living and forge a new path that embraces sustainability, self-sufficiency, and a harmonious relationship with the natural world.

As individuals navigate this decision-making process, they find themselves at the intersection of ideals and realities. The romanticized notion of off-grid living is met with practical implementation challenges. Yet, within this convergence lies the potential for personal growth, resilience, and a deepened connection with the environment. The decision to go off-grid is not merely a lifestyle choice; it is a profound statement about the values that guide one's life and the commitment to crafting a future that is both sustainable and fulfilling.

CHAPTER II

Essential Off-Grid Skills

Basic Survival Skills

In off-grid living, acquiring basic survival skills is not just a practical necessity but a fundamental aspect of embracing a lifestyle that champions self-sufficiency and resilience. These skills form the bedrock upon which off- grid dwellers build their capacity to navigate the challenges of living independently, away from the safety nets of urban infrastructure. From crafting makeshift shelters to sourcing and purifying water, mastering basic survival skills becomes an art that connects individuals to the primal essence of human existence.

At the heart of these skills lies the ability to adapt to the unpredictability of the natural environment. Off-grid living often means residing in remote locations where nature, while stunningly beautiful, can be unforgiving. Individuals choosing this lifestyle recognize the importance of understanding the lay of the land, recognizing edible plants, and identifying potential hazards. Navigational skills, honed through map reading and orienteering, become crucial tools for off-grid dwellers as they traverse terrains that are not just physical but metaphoric expressions of their journey toward self-sufficiency.

Building a shelter is one of the first and foremost survival skills that off-grid dwellers must master. Unlike the pre-constructed homes of urban living, off-grid shelters may need to be crafted from available natural materials. This skill involves understanding the properties of local flora, identifying suitable building materials, and constructing shelters that protect from the elements. The art of creating a home from the land not only speaks to practical survival but also embodies a profound connection to the environment.

Firecraft is another indispensable skill in the off-grid survival toolkit. Beyond the romantic allure of a crackling campfire, the ability to start and maintain a fire is a fundamental aspect of survival. Fire provides warmth in the cold, a means of cooking food, and a psychological anchor in the wilderness. Off-grid dwellers must become adept at fire-making techniques, whether using traditional methods like friction fire or modern tools like fire starters. The skill extends to fire safety, as individuals learn to manage and control fire to prevent unintended consequences in the wild.

Securing a safe and potable water source is a paramount survival skill. Off-grid living often means reliance on local water bodies, rainwater harvesting, or wells. Understanding water purification methods becomes crucial to ensure that water is free from contaminants. From boiling to filtration, off-grid dwellers must master techniques that transform raw water into a life-sustaining resource. This skill contributes to personal well-being and underscores the off-grid commitment to sustainable and responsible resource management.

Foraging and wild edibles knowledge are skills that bridge the gap between sustenance and the surrounding environment. Off-grid dwellers become attuned to the seasons, identifying plants that offer nourishment and medicinal benefits. This skill goes beyond mere survival; it encapsulates a holistic approach to living in harmony with the land. Foraging is a celebration of nature's abundance, transforming the act of gathering food into a profound connection with the cycles of life.

The ability to navigate and orient oneself in the wild is a skill that echoes the ancient instincts of human survival. In off-grid living, where GPS signals may be unreliable or inaccessible, individuals must rely on traditional navigation methods. Map reading, using a compass, and understanding natural landmarks become essential skills for off-grid dwellers exploring unfamiliar terrains. This skill ensures safe travels and deepens the connection to the landscape, fostering a sense of kinship with the Earth.

First aid proficiency is a non-negotiable aspect of off-grid survival. Individuals must be equipped to handle minor injuries and emergencies without immediate access to medical facilities. Basic first aid skills, including wound care, CPR, and natural remedies, empower off-grid dwellers to address health concerns effectively. This skill embodies the ethos of self-sufficiency, where individuals take responsibility for their well-being and that of their community.

In the context of off-grid living, self-defense skills gain a pragmatic significance. While the serene landscapes may depict tranquility, off-grid dwellers must be mindful of threats from wildlife or other humans. Learning self-defense techniques becomes a means of ensuring personal safety and security. This skill is not just about physical prowess; it reflects the broader commitment to creating a resilient and protected off-grid lifestyle.

The practice of minimal-impact camping is an extension of survival skills that underscores the off-grid ethos of leaving no trace. Individuals venture into the wilderness for camping or exploration, adopting practices that minimize their environmental impact. This includes responsible waste management, ethical foraging, and respecting the natural habitat. The skill of minimal-impact camping reflects a conscientious approach to enjoying nature without compromising its delicate balance.

The journey into mastering basic survival skills is not just about acquiring practical knowledge; it is a transformative process that shapes the mindset of off-grid dwellers. It cultivates a deep respect for the environment, a sense of responsibility for one's well-being, and a connection to the primal instincts that have guided human survival for millennia. Beyond the pragmatic aspects, these skills embody the spirit of self-sufficiency and resilience that define the off-grid lifestyle.

Yet, the acquisition of these skills has its challenges. The learning curve for mastering survival skills can be steep, especially for those accustomed to the conveniences of modern living. The initial discomfort of adapting to outdoor living, the physical demands of crafting shelters or foraging for food, and the mental fortitude required for navigation and self-defense can test the resolve of individuals new to off-grid living. However, within these challenges, the true essence of survival skills is revealed—a testament to human adaptability, tenacity, and the innate ability to thrive even in the wild terrain of self-sufficiency.

In conclusion, basic survival skills form the cornerstone of off-grid living, offering a roadmap for individuals seeking a lifestyle marked by self-sufficiency and resilience. These skills transcend the realm of practical knowledge, becoming a way of life that embodies a profound connection to the environment and a commitment to responsible living. As off-grid dwellers navigate the wild terrain of self-sufficiency, they embark on a transformative journey that ensures survival in the physical sense and fosters a deeper understanding of the intricate dance between humans and the natural world.

DIY Repairs and Maintenance

In the realm of off-grid living, the ability to perform DIY repairs and maintenance emerges as a crucial skill set beyond mere practicality—a testament to the ethos of self-sufficiency and resilience. Unlike the convenience of urban living, where professionals are a phone call away, off-grid dwellers find themselves in a paradigm where self-reliance is not just a preference but a necessity. Whether fixing a malfunctioning solar panel, repairing a water catchment system, or maintaining a sustainable shelter, DIY repairs and maintenance become a cornerstone of an independent lifestyle.

At the heart of this skill set lies the capacity to troubleshoot and problem-solve. Off-grid living often involves using alternative energy sources like solar or wind power. Diagnosing and repairing issues with these systems becomes vital for maintaining a consistent energy supply. Off-grid dwellers must become adept at identifying faults in wiring, understanding battery storage, and even calibrating solar panels to optimize energy production. This knowledge ensures the seamless functioning of off-grid infrastructure and empowers individuals to address challenges without reliance on external expertise.

The sustainable shelter that characterizes off-grid living demands constant attention and maintenance. Unlike traditional homes, often constructed with durable materials and backed by municipal services, off-grid shelters may utilize natural or recycled materials that require regular upkeep. DIY repairs involve fixing structural issues and adapting to the changing seasons. Off-grid dwellers must master the art of sealing leaks, insulating against temperature extremes, and repairing any wear and tear that may occur without immediate access to professional services.

Water catchment and purification systems represent another frontier where DIY repairs and maintenance skills come to the fore. Off-grid living often means relying on rainwater harvesting or local water sources; any disruption in these systems can have immediate consequences. Individuals must be proficient in fixing leaks, ensuring proper filtration, and maintaining water storage facilities. The ability to troubleshoot and repair these systems is not just about convenience; it is about securing a life-sustaining resource in an environment where water scarcity can be a real challenge.

The do-it-yourself ethos extends to off-grid kitchens, where sustainable cooking and food preservation methods require hands-on attention. Off-grid dwellers often adopt alternative cooking methods, such as solar ovens or rocket stoves, which necessitate regular maintenance. DIY repairs may involve adjusting reflectors on a solar oven, replacing parts in a rocket stove, or improvising cooking solutions based on available resources. Moreover, food preservation techniques, from canning to dehydrating, demand a skillful balance of temperature control and resourceful problem-solving.

Beyond the technical aspects, the art of DIY repairs and maintenance embodies a mindset that values resourcefulness and adaptability. Off-grid dwellers must cultivate the ability to repurpose materials, improvise solutions, and think creatively in the face of challenges. The limitations of off-grid living, far from being constraints, become opportunities for innovation. The journey of maintaining an independent lifestyle becomes a continuous learning process that hones problem-solving skills and instills a sense of confidence in the face of adversity.

One of the fundamental advantages of DIY repairs and maintenance in off-grid living is its cost-effectiveness. In the absence of immediate access to professional services, off-grid dwellers may find that self-reliance addresses issues promptly and eliminates the financial burden associated with hiring external help. The savings accumulated by mastering the art of DIY repairs can be significant over the long term, reinforcing the economic sustainability hallmark of the off-grid lifestyle.

Moreover, the capacity for DIY repairs fosters a deeper connection between individuals and their living environment. Off-grid dwellers, intimately involved in maintaining their homes and systems, develop a profound understanding of the intricacies of sustainable living. This hands-on engagement with the physical aspects of off-grid infrastructure builds a sense of ownership and stewardship. Repairing and maintaining becomes a ritual that strengthens the bond between individuals and the structures that support their independent lifestyles.

While the advantages of DIY repairs and maintenance in off-grid living are evident, the journey is challenging. Acquiring the necessary skills requires ongoing learning, especially for those new to DIY repairs. The initial discomfort of grappling with unfamiliar systems, the learning curve associated with electrical work or plumbing, and the potential for trial and error demand patience and perseverance. However, within these challenges, the true essence of self-sufficiency is revealed—a journey of continuous growth and empowerment.

The significance of the DIY ethos extends beyond the immediate practicalities of repairs and maintenance; it permeates the broader narrative of off-grid living. It embodies the resilience required to thrive in a self-sustained lifestyle, where challenges are not seen as obstacles but as opportunities for skill development. The act of repairing and maintaining becomes a celebration of human ingenuity and adaptability, reflecting the essence of living off the grid.

In conclusion, DIY repairs and maintenance are integral to the off-grid lifestyle, offering a pathway to self-sufficiency and resilience. This skill set encompasses a wide range of practical knowledge, from troubleshooting energy systems to fixing structural issues in sustainable shelters. Beyond the technical aspects, the art of DIY repairs embodies a mindset that values creativity, resourcefulness, and adaptability. The journey of maintaining an independent lifestyle becomes not just a practical necessity but a continuous exploration of human potential. As off-grid dwellers master the art of DIY repairs, they confidently navigate the terrain of self-sufficiency, reinforcing the ethos that defines their unique way of life.

Resourceful Cooking and Food Preservation Techniques

In the tapestry of off-grid living, resourceful cooking, and food preservation techniques emerge as both an art and a necessity. Unlike the convenience of urban kitchens, off-grid cooking demands ingenuity beyond traditional recipes and modern appliances. Whether harnessing solar ovens, crafting improvised rocket stoves, or preserving seasonal harvests without refrigeration, the culinary journey in off-grid living becomes a testament to resourcefulness and sustainable practices.

Off-grid cooking begins with a mindful selection of energy sources. Embracing renewable energy is a core principle of sustainable living, and off-grid dwellers often opt for solar or wind-powered cooking methods. Solar ovens harness the power of the sun to cook meals, using reflective surfaces to concentrate sunlight onto a cooking chamber. The simplicity of this technology aligns with the off-grid ethos, allowing individuals to cook without relying on non-renewable resources. Similarly, rocket stoves, which burn small amounts of wood efficiently, are famous for off-grid cooking, balancing fuel efficiency and minimal environmental impact.

The resourceful off-grid kitchen extends beyond energy sources to encompass alternative cooking appliances. Dutch ovens, cast-iron skillets, and clay pots become staple tools capable of withstanding the rigors of off-grid cooking. These durable and versatile vessels allow for various cooking methods, from baking to slow simmering, while fighting the test of time without immediate access to commercial kitchen equipment. Off-grid dwellers become adept at adapting traditional recipes to these vessels, embracing the rustic charm of off-grid cooking.

Preserving the bounty of seasonal harvests is a central aspect of off-grid living, where refrigeration may be limited or unavailable. Canning, a time-honored preservation method, becomes a vital skill for off-grid dwellers. Whether it's tomatoes, fruits, or pickled vegetables, canning allows individuals to store and enjoy abundant harvest throughout the year. The process involves sealing food in sterilized jars, creating a vacuum that inhibits the growth of microorganisms. This method not only preserves the nutritional value of the food but also reduces waste and reliance on store-bought produce.

Dehydrating is another resourceful technique that off-grid dwellers employ to extend the shelf life of food. Individuals create lightweight, space-efficient, and long-lasting provisions by removing moisture from fruits, vegetables, and even meats. Dehydrated foods can be rehydrated with water, cooked directly, or enjoyed as nutritious snacks. This technique is precious for off-grid living, where storage space may be limited, and the ability to preserve food without refrigeration is a crucial consideration.

Fermentation, a traditional method of food preservation, takes center stage in the off-grid kitchen. From sauerkraut to kimchi, off-grid dwellers harness the power of beneficial bacteria to transform raw ingredients into flavorful and probiotic-rich delights. Fermented foods contribute to gut health and offer a unique and resourceful way to preserve vegetables without the need for refrigeration. The art of fermentation becomes a culinary adventure, allowing individuals to experiment with flavors and techniques handed down through generations.

Off-grid cooking also embraces the ethos of zero waste. Scraps and peels that may be discarded in traditional kitchens find new life in off-grid recipes. Vegetable scraps become the base for nutrient-rich broths, while fruit peels may be dehydrated to create zesty dish additions. The resourceful off-grid kitchen transforms every ingredient into an opportunity for creativity, reducing waste and maximizing the utility of available resources.

Foraging and wild edibles knowledge further enriches the off-grid culinary repertoire. Off-grid dwellers become attuned to the seasonal availability of edible plants in their surroundings. Nettles, dandelions, and wild mushrooms are just a few examples of the diverse array of foraged foods that find their way into off-grid dishes. The ability to identify, harvest, and incorporate wild edibles enhances the variety of flavors in off-grid meals and reinforces the connection between individuals and the natural environment.

In addition to the creative and sustainable aspects, off- grid cooking is an exercise in meal planning and preparation. Off-grid dwellers often adopt batch cooking techniques, preparing more significant quantities of meals that can be stored and reheated. This approach minimizes the daily energy consumption required for cooking and ensures a steady supply of ready-to-eat meals. The resourceful off-grid kitchen becomes a strategic space where efficiency and sustainability converge to create nourishing and flavorful dishes.

While the resourceful off-grid kitchen excels in sustainable cooking and food preservation, it has challenges. Relating to alternative energy sources and traditional cooking methods may demand a shift in culinary habits and techniques. Individuals must learn to adapt recipes to the limitations of off-grid cooking appliances, exploring the nuances of temperature control and cooking times. The absence of immediate access to a wide range of ingredients may also prompt off-grid dwellers to embrace a more seasonal and locally sourced approach to cooking.

Moreover, the off-grid kitchen requires a commitment to ongoing learning and experimentation. The art of resourceful cooking involves a continuous exploration of techniques, flavors, and adaptations. Off-grid dwellers must become adept at improvising solutions, whether adjusting cooking times based on the weather or crafting makeshift utensils from available materials. This culinary journey embodies the essence of off-grid living—a dynamic and ever-evolving dance with the elements and the resources at hand.

In conclusion, resourceful cooking and food preservation techniques in off-grid living encapsulate the spirit of self-sufficiency, sustainability, and creativity. The off-grid kitchen becomes a canvas for culinary exploration, where individuals harness alternative energy sources, traditional cooking methods, and preservation techniques to create nourishing meals. The resourceful off-grid kitchen extends beyond practicality to embody a deeper connection with the environment, a commitment to zero waste, and a celebration of nature's abundance. As off-grid dwellers master the art of resourceful cooking, they not only satisfy their nutritional needs but also contribute to a way of life that embraces ingenuity, sustainability, and a profound connection with past culinary traditions.

CHAPTER III

Off-Grid Energy Solutions

Solar Power Systems

In the realm of off-grid living, where the hum of city electricity is replaced by the whispers of nature, solar power systems stand as silent sentinels, capturing the sun's energy to illuminate a sustainable way of life. The harnessing of solar power is not merely a technological feat; it is a fundamental shift in the paradigm of energy consumption, embodying the ethos of self-sufficiency, environmental stewardship, and resilience. As off-grid dwellers embrace the silent revolution of solar energy, they embark on a journey that powers their homes and illuminates the path to a more sustainable and intentional existence.

At the heart of the solar power system is the photovoltaic (PV) cell, a marvel of engineering that converts sunlight into electricity. These cells, typically composed of silicon, generate direct current (DC) electricity when exposed to sunlight. The solar panels comprising interconnected PV cells become the primary building blocks of an off-grid solar power system. The simplicity of this process belies its transformative potential as off-grid dwellers transition from dependence on centralized power grids to generating their electricity locally, on-site, and from a renewable source.

The installation of solar panels marks a pivotal moment in the off-grid journey. Placed strategically to capture maximum sunlight, these panels become the silent harbingers of energy independence. Off-grid dwellers often adopt a combination of fixed and tracking solar panels, the latter adjusting their position throughout the day to follow the sun's trajectory. This dynamic alignment enhances energy production, ensuring that off-grid homes are bathed in the glow of sustainable power.

The captured solar energy undergoes a crucial transformation through inverters, which convert DC electricity into alternating current (AC), the standard form of home electricity. This conversion enables off-grid dwellers to power household appliances, charge electronic devices, and illuminate their homes with the energy harnessed from the sun. Batteries play a vital role in the solar power system, storing excess energy generated during sunny periods for use during cloudy days or nighttime. This storage capacity ensures a consistent power supply, bridging the gap between intermittent sunlight and the continuous energy demand.

One of the defining features of solar power systems in off-grid living is the modularity and scalability they offer. Off-grid dwellers can tailor their solar setups to meet their specific energy needs. As the demand for power increases or additional appliances are introduced, the solar power system can be expanded by adding more panels and batteries. This flexibility allows individuals to adapt their energy infrastructure over time, ensuring that it aligns with the evolving requirements of their off-grid lifestyle.

The economic benefits of solar power systems extend beyond the initial investment. While the setup costs for solar panels and inverters may constitute a substantial upfront expense, the long-term savings on utility bills become a testament to the financial sustainability of off-grid living. The absence of monthly electricity bills and the potential for government incentives or tax credits further reinforce the economic viability of solar power. Off-grid dwellers find themselves not just consumers of energy but producers, with the potential to achieve energy autonomy and recoup their initial investment over the years.

Yet, the transition to solar power has its challenges. The initial setup costs, although offset by long-term savings, can be a barrier for some individuals considering the shift to off-grid living. The learning curve associated with installing and maintaining solar power systems may also pose challenges for those unfamiliar with the technology. However, within these challenges, the true essence of off-grid living is revealed—an ongoing commitment to learning, adaptability, and the pursuit of a lifestyle that prioritizes sustainability over convenience.

Beyond the economic considerations, adopting solar power systems in off-grid living embodies a profound commitment to environmental stewardship. Solar energy is a clean and renewable resource, free from the greenhouse gas emissions associated with fossil fuels. The decentralized nature of solar power generation reduces transmission losses, making it an environmentally responsible choice. By choosing solar energy, off-grid dwellers become active participants in the global effort to mitigate climate change, demonstrating that sustainable living is not merely an individual choice but a collective responsibility.

The environmental impact of solar power systems extends to the conservation of natural resources. Unlike traditional energy sources that require the extraction and combustion of finite fossil fuels, solar power relies on the boundless energy of the sun. Reducing dependence on non-renewable resources contributes to preserving ecosystems, biodiversity, and the delicate balance of the planet. By embracing solar energy, off-grid dwellers participate in a regenerative cycle that aligns with the rhythms of nature.

The aesthetics of solar panels have become an integral part of the off-grid landscape. Rather than being an intrusive addition, these panels merge seamlessly with the natural surroundings, capturing sunlight without disrupting the visual harmony of the environment. Integrating solar technology with off-grid homes becomes a statement—an embodiment of the symbiotic relationship between human habitation and the natural world. Off-grid dwellers often find creative ways to incorporate solar panels into their architectural designs, further enhancing the visual appeal of sustainable living.

The evolution of solar power technology continues to shape the landscape of off-grid living. Advancements in energy storage, efficiency, and affordability enhance the feasibility of solar power systems for a broader audience. Off-grid dwellers are at the forefront of this technological wave, embracing innovations that optimize their energy infrastructure. From smart inverters to efficient battery technologies, the integration of cutting-edge solutions ensures that off-grid solar power systems remain at the pinnacle of sustainable energy practices.

In conclusion, solar power systems stand as beacons of sustainability in the world of off-grid living, illuminating a path toward energy independence, environmental stewardship, and resilience. Integrating solar panels, inverters, and batteries transforms off-grid homes into self-sufficient havens powered by the sun. The economic viability, environmental responsibility, and technological advancements associated with solar power systems make them integral components of the off-grid lifestyle. As off-grid dwellers harness the sun's energy, they not only illuminate their homes but also contribute to a future where sustainable living is not just a choice but a necessity for the planet's well-being.

Wind Turbines and Hydro Power

In the expansive canvas of off-grid living, where the quest for sustainable energy sources takes center stage, the gentle whispers of the wind and the rhythmic flow of water emerge as potent allies. Wind turbines and hydropower, harnessed through innovative technologies, become the harbingers of energy independence, offering off-grid dwellers a dynamic and renewable alternative to traditional grid-based electricity. Drawing from the elemental forces of nature, these solutions embody the spirit of self-sufficiency, environmental harmony, and resilience, ushering in a new era of off-grid energy exploration.

Wind turbines, towering sentinels that gracefully spin with the wind's caress, capture kinetic energy and convert it into electricity. These modern marvels, often installed strategically in locations with consistent wind patterns, represent a sustainable alternative to conventional power sources. The basic design involves rotor blades that rotate with the wind, driving a generator to produce electrical power. The simplicity of this mechanism belies its transformative potential, as off-grid dwellers embrace the rhythmic dance between wind and turbine to generate clean and renewable energy.

Installing wind turbines in off-grid living is a strategic endeavor guided by understanding local wind patterns and topography. Off-grid dwellers often conduct thorough assessments to determine the optimal placement for turbines, ensuring maximum exposure to prevailing winds. The tower's height is also critical, allowing the turbine to tap into higher wind speeds that prevail at elevated altitudes. This intentional positioning transforms the wind turbine into a sculptural beacon, not just capturing energy but embodying the synergy between human habitation and the elemental forces of the environment.

The energy harvested by wind turbines transforms power electronics, converting the variable voltage produced by the turbine into a consistent and usable form. Inverters play a crucial role in this process, ensuring that the electricity generated aligns with the requirements of off-grid homes. The integration of energy storage solutions, such as batteries, further enhances the reliability of wind power systems, enabling off-grid dwellers to store excess energy for use during periods of low wind or increased demand.

Hydropower, another stalwart in the off-grid energy arsenal, harnesses the kinetic energy of flowing water to generate electricity. The fundamental principle involves converting potential energy in elevated water bodies like rivers or streams into kinetic energy through turbines. As water flows over the turbines, the mechanical energy is translated into electrical power, offering off-grid dwellers a continuous and renewable energy source. Small-scale hydropower systems, often called micro-hydro systems, are prevalent in off-grid settings due to their adaptability and efficiency.

The design and implementation of micro-hydro systems in off-grid living entail considering the nearby natural water features. Off-grid dwellers identify suitable locations where the terrain allows water diversion to drive turbines. The sizing of the system is calibrated to match the flow rate and elevation drop of the water source, optimizing the conversion of water's potential energy into electricity. The integration of control systems ensures that the power generated aligns with the dynamic nature of water flow, creating a harmonious relationship between the micro-hydro system and the surrounding landscape.

One of the defining features of wind turbines and hydropower systems is their complementarity with solar power. Off-grid dwellers often adopt hybrid energy solutions that combine these renewable sources to create a robust and reliable energy infrastructure. The intermittent nature of solar power, influenced by weather and daylight hours, finds a natural counterpart in the continuous and often consistent energy production of wind and hydro systems. The synergy between these elements ensures a steady power supply, mitigating the challenges associated with reliance on a single energy source.

The economic considerations of wind turbines and hydropower systems in off-grid living extend beyond the initial setup costs. While the investment in turbines, towers, and control systems may constitute a significant upfront expense, the long-term savings on utility bills and the potential for government incentives or tax credits contribute to the financial sustainability of these systems. By diversifying their energy sources, off-grid dwellers reduce their dependence on external power grids, reinforcing their commitment to financial autonomy and energy resilience.

From an environmental perspective, wind turbines and hydropower systems embody the principles of sustainability and conservation. Both sources produce electricity without emitting greenhouse gases or relying on finite resources. Wind energy, derived from the kinetic energy of moving air, is a clean and renewable alternative to fossil fuels. Similarly, hydropower, tapping into the gravitational potential energy of flowing water, offers a consistent and environmentally friendly option for off-grid living. The integration of these systems aligns with the broader goal of reducing carbon footprints and contributing to a more ecologically balanced way of life.

The visual impact of wind turbines and micro-hydro systems becomes integral to the off-grid landscape. Rather than being intrusive, these structures merge with the natural surroundings, creating a harmonious coexistence between technology and nature. The sight of wind turbines gracefully turning in the breeze or the gentle hum of a micro-hydro system nestled in a flowing stream becomes a visual and auditory testament to the off-grid commitment to sustainable living. Off-grid dwellers often take pride in integrating these elements, transforming them into functional components and aesthetic expressions of their environmental values.

While wind turbines and hydropower systems offer compelling advantages, their adoption in off-grid living is challenging. The variability of wind speeds and water flow rates demands careful planning and consideration of local conditions. Off-grid dwellers must conduct thorough assessments to determine the feasibility of these systems in their specific locations. The initial investment in equipment and installation may pose a financial barrier for some individuals, requiring a thoughtful evaluation of long-term benefits against upfront costs.

Moreover, integrating wind turbines and micro-hydro systems necessitates a commitment to ongoing maintenance. Off-grid dwellers must monitor and address wear and tear on turbine blades, inspect electrical components, and ensure that control systems function optimally. The dynamic nature of wind and water requires a proactive approach to system management involving regular checks and adjustments. However, within these challenges, the true essence of off-grid living is revealed—a journey of continuous learning, adaptability, and a deepened connection with the elemental forces that power sustainable living.

In conclusion, wind turbines and hydropower systems are formidable allies in the off-grid quest for sustainable energy. The turbine blades' graceful rotation and the rhythmic hum of the flowing water embody the harmony between human habitation and the elements. Drawing from the renewable forces of wind and water, these systems illuminate a path toward energy independence, environmental stewardship, and resilience. As off-grid dwellers embrace the dance between technology and nature, they power their homes and contribute to a future where the quest for energy aligns with the planet's rhythms.

Energy Storage and Management

In the realm of off-grid living, where the ebb and flow of energy are intimately connected to the whims of nature, the art of energy storage and management emerges as a critical facet of sustainability. The quest for self- sufficiency and resilience in off-grid settings hinges on capturing, storing, and judiciously managing the energy harvested from renewable sources. From the silent hum of batteries storing solar power to the intricate dance of control systems optimizing energy usage, the landscape of off-grid living is shaped by the delicate interplay between energy storage and management, offering a blueprint for a more intentional and sustainable lifestyle.

At the heart of energy storage in off-grid living are batteries, silent powerhouses that store the harvested energy for use during periods of low production or high demand. These batteries, often deep-cycle and designed for renewable energy systems, come in various chemistries such as lead-acid, lithium-ion, and advanced gel technologies. The selection of batteries is a crucial consideration in off-grid setups, balancing factors such as capacity, cycle life, and maintenance requirements. As solar panels or wind turbines generate electricity, surplus energy is directed to charge these batteries, creating a reservoir that ensures a continuous power supply even when the primary energy sources are unavailable.

Managing stored energy in off-grid living involves a symphony of control systems, inverters, and monitoring tools. Inverters are pivotal in converting the direct current (DC) stored in batteries into alternating current (AC), the standard form of home electricity. Advanced inverters offer features such as grid synchronization and intelligent grid connectivity, enhancing the flexibility and compatibility of off-grid systems. Control systems, often integrated with inverters, govern the distribution and prioritization of energy usage, ensuring that essential appliances receive power when needed and that excess energy is stored for future use. Monitoring tools provide real-time insights into energy production, consumption, and storage, empowering off-grid dwellers to make informed decisions about their energy usage patterns.

The selection of an appropriate energy storage system is a strategic decision for off-grid dwellers, influenced by factors such as the availability of renewable resources, energy demands, and budget considerations. With their established technology and affordability, lead-acid batteries are commonly used in off-grid setups. Lithium-ion batteries, known for their high energy density and longer cycle life, offer a more compact and lightweight alternative. Gel batteries, with their maintenance-free design and resistance to deep discharges, find favor in off-grid applications where reliability is paramount. The choice of battery technology becomes a nuanced decision, balancing performance metrics with the specific requirements of the off-grid lifestyle.

Beyond batteries, off-grid dwellers explore innovative energy storage solutions that align with sustainability principles. Compressed air energy storage, for example, captures surplus energy by compressing air into storage containers. When electricity is needed, the compressed air is released to drive turbines and generate power. Similarly, flywheel energy storage systems store kinetic energy in spinning flywheels, releasing it when needed to provide instantaneous power. These emerging technologies offer alternatives or supplements to traditional battery-based storage, providing off-grid dwellers with a diverse toolkit for managing their energy needs.

The management of energy storage extends beyond the technical components to encompass a mindset of efficiency and conservation. Off-grid dwellers adopt practices such as load shedding, where non-essential appliances are temporarily turned off during high-demand or low-energy production periods. This intentional approach to energy usage ensures that available power is directed towards essential needs, maximizing the longevity of stored energy. Timed usage of appliances, prioritizing energy-efficient technologies, and adopting energy-conscious habits become integral aspects of the off-grid lifestyle.

One of the challenges in energy storage for off-grid living is the balance between energy generation and consumption. The intermittent nature of renewable energy sources, such as sunlight or wind, requires careful planning to ensure a steady and reliable power supply. Overestimating or underestimating energy needs can lead to inefficiencies, impacting the overall viability of off-grid systems. Off-grid dwellers must conduct thorough energy audits, assessing the requirements of appliances, lighting, and other electrical devices to dimension their storage systems adequately. Adopting energy-efficient appliances and a conscious effort to minimize unnecessary energy consumption becomes a key strategy in achieving equilibrium between production and demand.

The economic considerations of energy storage in off-grid living involve the upfront costs of batteries and inverters and the long-term savings and sustainability benefits. While the initial investment in high-quality batteries may constitute a significant expense, these components' extended cycle life and reliability contribute to the financial viability of off-grid living over time. Off-grid dwellers often view energy storage as a long-term investment, recognizing that the autonomy and resilience gained outweigh the upfront costs. The reduction in reliance on external power grids, coupled with potential government incentives or tax credits, further reinforces the economic sustainability of energy storage in off-grid settings.

From an environmental perspective, adopting efficient energy storage aligns with sustainability principles and responsible resource management.

By capturing and storing energy from renewable sources, off-grid dwellers reduce their dependence on non-renewable resources and minimize their carbon footprint. Integrating energy storage with renewable energy systems transforms off- grid living into a regenerative cycle, where energy is harvested, stored, and utilized in harmony with the natural rhythms of the environment. This conscious approach to energy management contributes to the broader global effort to transition towards a more sustainable and ecologically balanced energy landscape.

The journey into energy storage and management in off-grid living is challenging. The technology involved requires understanding and expertise that may be unfamiliar to those transitioning from traditional grid-based living. Off-grid dwellers must become adept at monitoring and managing their energy systems, troubleshooting issues, and adapting to the dynamic nature of renewable energy production. The learning curve associated with efficient energy storage demands a commitment to ongoing education and a willingness to embrace a more conscious and intentional approach to energy usage.

Moreover, the dynamic nature of renewable energy sources introduces variability into the off-grid energy equation. Factors such as weather conditions, seasonal changes, and fluctuations in energy demand necessitate a proactive and adaptive mindset in energy management. Off-grid dwellers must be attuned to the nuances of their local environment, adjusting their energy usage patterns to align with the availability of sunlight, wind, or flowing water. This responsiveness becomes a fundamental aspect of the off-grid lifestyle, where individuals learn to navigate the ever-changing energy landscape with resilience and resourcefulness.

In conclusion, energy storage and management are pillars of sustainability in the world of off-grid living, shaping a lifestyle that is powered by renewable sources and guided by intentional and conscious energy practices. The silent hum of batteries storing solar power and the orchestrated dance of control systems optimizing energy usage become integral components of the off-grid experience. As off-grid dwellers master the art of energy storage and management, they not only sustain their homes but contribute to a future where the quest for energy aligns with the rhythms of nature, fostering a more harmonious and regenerative way of life.

CHAPTER IV

Sustainable Water Management

Rainwater Harvesting

In the tapestry of off-grid living, where sustainability and self-sufficiency are paramount, rainwater harvesting emerges as a cornerstone of resourceful water management. The gentle patter of raindrops becomes a source of liquid gold, captured and channeled to fulfill the diverse water needs of off-grid dwellers. This ancient practice, rooted in traditional societies' wisdom and the ingenuity of modern technology, transforms rainwater into a precious and sustainable resource. As off-grid communities embrace the delicate dance between clouds and earth, they embark on a journey that quenches their thirst and embodies the ethos of responsible and harmonious living.

Rainwater harvesting encompasses a spectrum of techniques designed to capture and store rainwater for various uses. The fundamental components of a rainwater harvesting system include catchment surfaces, conveyance systems, storage tanks, and distribution networks. The catchment surface, typically the roof of a dwelling or a specially designed collection area, is the first point of contact for raindrops. As rainwater flows over these surfaces, it is channeled through gutters and downspouts into storage tanks. These tanks, varying in size and material, become reservoirs for the collected rainwater, holding the key to a reliable and decentralized water supply in off-grid settings.

The utilization of rainwater in off-grid living extends to a range of applications, from household activities such as drinking, cooking, and bathing to agricultural irrigation and landscape maintenance. Filtration and purification systems are often integrated into rainwater harvesting setups to ensure the collected water meets the required quality standards. The simplicity of these systems belies their transformative impact, allowing off-grid dwellers to break free from dependence on centralized water sources and manage their water needs sustainably and efficiently.

Integrating rainwater harvesting into the off-grid lifestyle requires careful consideration of local climate conditions, water demand, and the scale of the system. Off-grid dwellers tailor their rainwater harvesting setups to match the architectural design of their homes, the size of their catchment surfaces, and the specific water needs of their households. Whether through traditional rain barrels or more sophisticated tank systems, the objective remains to capture and utilize rainwater that aligns with the principles of conservation and environmental responsibility.

Beyond the practical considerations, rainwater harvesting in off-grid living embodies a deeper connection with the natural environment. Off-grid dwellers become attuned to the seasonal rhythms of rainfall, adjusting their water usage patterns based on the ebb and flow of precipitation. Harvesting rainwater becomes a ritual, a dance with elements that foster a sense of responsibility and stewardship. In the face of climate variability and water scarcity, rainwater harvesting has become a technique and a philosophy—an affirmation of the delicate interdependence between human habitation and the natural world.

One of the primary advantages of rainwater harvesting in off-grid living is the reduction of reliance on external water sources. Off-grid communities, often in remote or rural locations, may need help accessing municipal water supplies. Drilling wells or transporting water over long distances can be impractical and resource-intensive. Rainwater harvesting offers a decentralized and on-site solution, empowering off-grid dwellers to create a sustainable water supply independent of external infrastructure. This autonomy enhances the resilience of off-grid communities and contributes to the broader goal of water conservation and responsible usage.

Moreover, rainwater harvesting aligns with water conservation principles, addressing the challenges posed by drought conditions and changing climate patterns. By capturing and utilizing rainwater, off-grid dwellers become active participants in the global effort to mitigate water scarcity. The decentralized nature of rainwater harvesting reduces the strain on existing water supplies and supports the regeneration of local aquifers. Through their collective commitment to responsible water management, off-grid communities demonstrate that sustainable living is not just a personal choice but a shared responsibility toward the planet's health.

The economic benefits of rainwater harvesting in off-grid living extend beyond the initial investment in collection and storage systems. While the setup costs may constitute a significant upfront expense, the long-term savings on water bills and the potential for government incentives or tax credits contribute to the financial sustainability of rainwater harvesting. By reducing their reliance on external water sources, off-grid dwellers not only cut down on recurring expenses but also insulate themselves from potential water shortages or price fluctuations. The economic viability of rainwater harvesting reinforces the financial autonomy that is a hallmark of the off-grid lifestyle.

The journey into rainwater harvesting in off-grid living is challenging. The variability of rainfall, influenced by climate conditions and seasonal changes, requires careful planning to ensure a reliable and consistent water supply. Off-grid dwellers must dimension their storage systems adequately, considering factors such as catchment area, storage capacity, and the frequency of rainfall. Adopting water-efficient appliances and a conscious effort to minimize unnecessary water consumption becomes a key strategy in achieving equilibrium between supply and demand.

Additionally, integrating rainwater harvesting demands a commitment to ongoing maintenance and monitoring. Storage tanks must be regularly inspected for debris or contaminants, and filtration systems should be maintained to ensure water quality. Off-grid dwellers become stewards of their rainwater harvesting systems, actively engaging in practices that optimize efficiency and sustainability. A thorough awareness of the local climate, the subtleties of collecting and storing water, and the adjustment of usage patterns to coincide with rainfall availability are all part of the learning curve that comes with rainwater harvesting.

In conclusion, rainwater harvesting is a testament to the resilience and resourcefulness of off-grid living, transforming raindrops into a sustainable and decentralized water supply. The rhythmic dance between clouds and catchment surfaces becomes a celebration of water as a precious resource that is conserved and utilized with intentionality and responsibility. As off-grid dwellers embrace the art and science of rainwater harvesting, they not only quench their thirst but also contribute to a future where water management aligns with the planet's rhythms, fostering a more harmonious and sustainable way of life.

Water Purification Methods

In the realm of off-grid living, where self-sufficiency and sustainability take center stage, the quest for pure and potable water is a paramount concern. The reliance on centralized water treatment facilities is often replaced by decentralized solutions that harness the abundance of nature. Being mindful of the delicate balance between human habitation and the environment, off-grid dwellers explore many water purification methods to transform local water sources into safe and drinkable liquid lifelines. From ancient techniques passed down through generations to cutting-edge technologies that harness the power of science, the landscape of water purification in off-grid living reflects a commitment to health, environmental stewardship, and resourceful living.

One of the time-honored methods of water purification in off-grid settings is boiling. This age-old practice, rooted in the wisdom of traditional societies, involves heating water to its boiling point to kill or inactivate harmful microorganisms. Boiling is simple yet effective, requiring minimal equipment—a heat source and a container. Off-grid dwellers, whether using open flames, stoves, or solar cookers, harness the power of heat to make water safe for consumption. While boiling effectively eliminates bacteria, viruses, and parasites, it may not remove chemical contaminants or sediment, necessitating additional purification methods for comprehensive water treatment.

Filtration is another cornerstone of water purification in off-grid living, offering a versatile and accessible solution. Filtration systems range from simple cloth filters to advanced ceramic or activated carbon filters. These mechanisms physically trap impurities, sediments, and microorganisms, allowing only clean water to pass through. Off-grid dwellers often integrate filtration systems into their water collection and storage setups, ensuring the water entering their homes is free from visible contaminants. The adaptability of filtration methods makes them suitable for various off-grid scenarios, from camping trips to remote homesteads.

Adopting modern water purification technologies in off-grid living introduces a spectrum of methods that leverage science and engineering to ensure water safety. For example, UV (ultraviolet) water purifiers use ultraviolet light to disrupt the DNA of microorganisms, rendering them incapable of reproduction. These compact and efficient devices are top-rated in off-grid settings, offering a rapid and chemical-free water disinfection method. Similarly, reverse osmosis systems utilize semipermeable membranes to remove impurities and contaminants from water, producing purified water for consumption. These advanced technologies provide off- grid dwellers a diverse toolkit for addressing water purification challenges.

Activated carbon is pivotal in many off-grid water purification methods, serving as a powerful adsorbent that captures impurities and chemicals. Activated carbon filters, commonly integrated into filtration systems, trap contaminants and improve water taste and odor. Charcoal, a natural form of activated carbon, has been used in traditional water purification methods for centuries. Off-grid communities often create makeshift charcoal filters, allowing water to percolate through layers of charcoal to enhance its quality. The porous nature of activated carbon makes it an effective medium for removing a broad range of pollutants, contributing to the comprehensive purification of off-grid water sources.

Iodine and chlorine tablets, while more chemical, find a place in the arsenal of water purification methods for off-grid dwellers. These tablets release disinfectants into the water, effectively killing bacteria and viruses. While their convenience and portability make them valuable for outdoor activities, off-grid communities may choose these methods as part of a multi-step purification process. However, it's important to note that the taste and odor of chemically treated water may be a consideration for some off-grid dwellers, prompting the exploration of additional methods to enhance the overall water quality.

Integrating natural materials and indigenous knowledge adds a cultural dimension to water purification in off-grid living. Sand filtration, for instance, draws from the ancient practice of using layers of sand to filter impurities from water. Off-grid dwellers construct sand filters, allowing water to percolate through various layers of sand and gravel to achieve a gradual purification process. Similarly, with their natural coagulant properties, moringa seeds have been utilized in some off-grid communities to clarify water by binding with impurities and sediments. These locally sourced and traditional methods underscore the resourcefulness and adaptability inherent in off-grid living.

Rainwater harvesting, a common practice in off-grid communities, introduces a unique dimension to water purification. Collecting rainwater is an initial step in the purification process, as rainwater is naturally free from many contaminants. Off-grid dwellers often integrate first flush systems, diverters, and mesh filters into their rainwater harvesting setups to prevent debris and contaminants from entering storage tanks. This conscious and integrated approach aligns with the off-grid ethos of using natural processes to enhance water quality.

The selection of water purification methods in off-grid living is guided by factors such as the quality of the water source, local climate conditions, and the community's specific needs. Off-grid dwellers conduct thorough assessments of their water sources, testing for contaminants and understanding the unique challenges associated with each location. The choice of purification methods becomes a nuanced decision involving a combination of techniques to ensure comprehensive water treatment. Off-grid communities often adopt a multi-barrier approach, combining filtration, disinfection, and other methods to create a robust and reliable water purification system.

The economic considerations of water purification in off-grid living extend beyond the upfront costs of equipment and technologies. While the initial investment in purification systems may constitute a significant expense, the long-term savings on potential medical costs, water treatment facilities, and the environmental impact of bottled water contribute to the financial sustainability of off-grid water purification. Off-grid dwellers, by taking ownership of their water purification methods, not only reduce their reliance on external infrastructure but also make a tangible contribution to the conservation of water resources.

From an environmental perspective, exploring water purification methods aligns with sustainability principles and responsible resource management. By harnessing natural processes and minimizing chemical treatments, off-grid dwellers reduce their ecological footprint and contribute to the preservation of ecosystems. The decentralized nature of off-grid water purification mitigates the strain on centralized treatment facilities and supports the regeneration of local water sources. Off-grid communities, through their commitment to responsible water management, embody a harmonious relationship between human needs and the planet's ecological balance.

The journey into water purification in off-grid living is challenging. The dynamic nature of water sources, influenced by seasonal changes, weather conditions, and human activities, demands continuous monitoring and adaptation. Off-grid dwellers must be attuned to the nuances of their local environment, adjusting their purification methods to align with the specific challenges presented by their water sources. The commitment to ongoing maintenance, regular testing, and the exploration of new purification technologies reflects the resourcefulness and adaptability that define the off-grid lifestyle.

In conclusion, water purification in off-grid living is a tapestry woven with threads of tradition, innovation, and environmental responsibility. From the ancient practice of boiling to the cutting-edge technologies of UV purification, off-grid dwellers navigate a diverse landscape of methods to ensure the safety and quality of their water. As they draw from the wisdom of the past and embrace the advancements of the present, off-grid communities not only quench their thirst but also contribute to a future where water purification aligns with the rhythms of nature, fostering a more resilient, sustainable, and conscious way of life.

Efficient Water Usage

In the intricate dance between human existence and the environment, water conservation and responsible management stand as cardinal virtues, especially in the realm of off-grid living. The ethos of self-sufficiency and sustainability inherent in off-grid communities spotlight the judicious use of water resources. Off-grid dwellers, aware of the delicate balance between human needs and environmental stewardship, embark on a journey of efficient water usage that transcends mere conservation —it becomes a philosophy, a way of life that nurtures the sustenance of both the individual and the planet.

Efficient water usage in off-grid living begins with a profound understanding of local water sources. Off-grid dwellers conduct meticulous assessments of their surroundings, gaining insights into the seasonal variations, natural flows, and overall health of water bodies. This intimate knowledge becomes the foundation for efficient water usage strategies. Whether drawing from wells, rivers, or rainwater harvesting systems, off-grid communities tailor their water usage patterns to align with the availability and dynamics of their local water sources.

The architecture of off-grid homes plays a pivotal role in efficient water usage. Integrating water-efficient appliances, fixtures, and plumbing systems becomes a cornerstone of off-grid design. Low-flow faucets, showerheads, and toilets reduce water consumption without compromising functionality. Greywater systems, designed to capture and reuse water from activities like washing dishes or showering, further amplify the efficiency of water usage. Off-grid dwellers embrace the principle that every drop counts, transforming their homes into models of water-conscious living.

Beyond technological solutions, off-grid communities foster a culture of mindfulness and awareness regarding water usage. Conscious behaviors become ingrained in daily life, such as shutting off faucets when unused, quickly repairing leaks, and abstaining from wasteful activities. Using efficient water extends to outdoor spaces, where permaculture and xeriscaping principles guide landscaping decisions. Off-grid dwellers select drought-resistant plants, implement rainwater harvesting for irrigation, and create a harmonious balance between human habitation and the natural landscape.

Rainwater harvesting, a common practice in off-grid living, exemplifies the marriage of efficiency and sustainability. The very act of capturing rainwater acknowledges the seasonal abundance of this precious resource. Off-grid dwellers utilize first flush systems, mesh filters, and storage tanks to maximize the efficiency of rainwater collection. This decentralized approach to water sourcing reduces the reliance on external water supplies and aligns with the principles of conservation and self-sufficiency.

Efficient water usage in off-grid living embraces the concept of water multiplicity, wherein a single source serves multiple purposes through careful design and planning. Greywater, for example, becomes a valuable resource that nourishes plants, supports irrigation, or even replenishes local ecosystems. Off-grid dwellers implement decentralized treatment and distribution systems for greywater, elevating it from a byproduct to a valuable component of a closed-loop water cycle. The integration of water multiplicity reduces waste, optimizes available resources, and fosters a holistic approach to water management.

Water conservation in off-grid living extends beyond individual households to the broader community. Shared water resources, such as community wells or rainwater harvesting systems, become collaborative endeavors where efficiency is a collective responsibility. Off-grid communities establish water usage guidelines, regularly maintain shared systems, and engage in educational initiatives to promote water-conscious practices. The sense of community ownership strengthens the resilience of water infrastructure and underscores the interconnectedness of individual actions with the well-being of the entire community.

Efficient water usage in off-grid living is intricately tied to regenerative design principles. Off-grid dwellers view water not as a finite commodity but as a dynamic force that sustains life. Permaculture principles, emphasizing the integration of human activities with natural ecosystems, guide the design of water systems that mimic the efficiency and resilience of natural cycles. Swales, berms, and contouring techniques become tools in the regenerative toolkit, capturing and directing water in ways that benefit both the landscape and the community.

The economic considerations of efficient water usage in off-grid living extend beyond the immediate cost savings on water bills. While off-grid dwellers may not be tethered to municipal water supplies, the financial sustainability of their lifestyle is intricately linked to the efficient use of available resources. The investment in water-efficient technologies, coupled with the long-term savings on maintenance and potential environmental costs, reinforces the economic viability of off-grid living. The ethos of efficiency extends to resource management, aligning with the broader principles of financial autonomy and sustainable living.

From an environmental perspective, the commitment to efficient water usage in off-grid living aligns with the urgent need for global water conservation. Off-grid communities, often residing in ecologically sensitive areas, become custodians of local water ecosystems. The reduction of water consumption, the avoidance of pollution, and the promotion of regenerative water practices contribute to the preservation of aquatic habitats and biodiversity. By embracing efficiency as a guiding principle, off-grid dwellers foster a more harmonious relationship between human habitation and the ecosystems that sustain life.

A few obstacles to off-grid water efficiency are the unpredictability of water supplies, the effects of climate change, and the requirement for ongoing adaptation. Off-grid dwellers navigate the ebb and flow of water availability, adjusting their habits and systems to align with seasonal changes and evolving conditions. The pursuit of efficiency demands a commitment to ongoing education, technological innovation, and a willingness to adapt to the dynamic nature of water resources. Within these challenges, the resilience and resourcefulness of off-grid living are revealed—a journey of continuous learning, adaptation, and a deepened connection with the natural world.

In conclusion, efficient water usage in off-grid living transcends the realm of conservation—it becomes a philosophy that shapes a way of life. From integrating water-efficient technologies to nurturing conscious habits, off-grid dwellers embody the principles of sustainability, self-sufficiency, and environmental stewardship. As they navigate the delicate dance between human needs and natural resources, they sustain their own lives and contribute to a future where efficient water usage is not just a choice but a necessity for the planet's well-being.

CHAPTER V

Eco-Friendly Shelter

Building with Natural Materials

In the realm of off-grid living, the choice of building materials is a transformative expression of a commitment to sustainability, self-sufficiency, and environmental harmony. Building with natural materials, a practice deeply rooted in traditional wisdom and ecological consciousness becomes a hallmark of the off-grid lifestyle. The dance between human habitation and the natural world takes center stage as off-grid dwellers embark on a journey to construct homes that shelter and harmonize with the surrounding landscape. From the earthy embrace of mud structures to the enduring strength of timber, using natural materials becomes a narrative that weaves together tradition, innovation, and a profound connection to the planet.

In various forms, mud is one of the oldest and most versatile building materials embraced by off-grid communities. Cob, adobe, and rammed earth are manifestations of the ancient art of building with mud, each technique carrying its unique characteristics and benefits. Cob, a blend of clay, sand, and straw, lends itself to sculptural forms and organic shapes, allowing off-grid dwellers to craft homes that blend seamlessly with the land's natural contours. Adobe, composed of sun-dried clay bricks, offers a simple and accessible construction method, capturing the warmth and authenticity of vernacular architecture. Rammed earth, where layers of earth are compacted to form solid walls, provides thermal mass and structural stability, creating extraordinary summer homes and warm winter homes. The use of mud in off-grid construction not only honors ancient building traditions but also celebrates this humble material's inherent beauty and sustainability.

Timber, another elemental building material, is a timeless companion to off-grid living. Sourcing timber from sustainably managed forests aligns with the principles of responsible resource use, ensuring that the ecological balance is maintained. Off-grid dwellers often use selective harvesting or salvaged timber, turning fallen trees or reclaimed wood into structural elements that tell a story of resilience and regeneration. Timber framing, a traditional construction technique showcasing wood's strength and versatility, has become a hallmark of off- grid architecture. The open, airy spaces created by timber framing echo the interconnectedness of the built environment with the natural surroundings, fostering a sense of continuity and unity.

Straw bale construction, a modern expression of natural building, combines the benefits of agricultural byproducts and passive design principles. Bales of straw, a byproduct of grain cultivation, are stacked and plastered to create walls that offer exceptional insulation and thermal performance. Straw bale homes, often characterized by their thick walls and sculptural curves, offer off-grid dwellers an innovative and energy-efficient alternative to conventional construction. The integration of natural plasters, made from clay, lime, or earthen materials, further enhances the ecological footprint of straw bale buildings, creating homes that breathe and age gracefully with time.

Using natural materials in off-grid construction extends beyond walls and roofs to embrace flooring, finishes, and insulation. Earthen floors, crafted from a mixture of clay, sand, and fibers, create durable but also tactile and warm surfaces. Natural finishes, such as clay or lime plaster, adorn walls with textures reflecting light and shadow, inviting a sensory connection to the built environment. Insulation materials, ranging from straw and cellulose to wool and recycled denim, prioritize thermal performance while minimizing the environmental impact. Off-grid dwellers embrace the holistic integration of natural materials, creating homes with a sense of authenticity, ecological mindfulness, and a deep reverence for the materials themselves.

The advantages of building with natural materials in off-grid living are multifaceted. From an environmental perspective, using materials such as mud, timber, and straw bales contributes to a reduced carbon footprint compared to conventional construction methods. The embodied energy—the total energy required to extract, process, transport, and install building materials—is significantly lower for natural materials, aligning with sustainability principles and responsible resource use. By choosing materials with minimal environmental impact, off-grid dwellers become stewards of the land, nurturing a built environment that treads lightly on the planet.

The thermal performance of natural materials adds another layer of resilience to off-grid homes. With their high thermal mass, mud structures regulate indoor temperatures by absorbing and slowly releasing heat. This inherent property creates homes that remain cool in summer and warm in winter, reducing the reliance on external heating and cooling systems. With its natural insulating properties, Timber enhances the energy efficiency of off-grid dwellings, creating comfortable living spaces that respond harmoniously to the local climate. Integrating natural plasters, finishes, and insulation materials further contributes to building homes by prioritizing comfort, health, and a balanced relationship with the natural elements.

The aesthetic appeal of natural materials in off-grid construction transcends the boundaries of mere functionality. Mud walls, with their earthy tones and textured surfaces, evoke a sense of groundedness and connection to the land. Whether exposed or concealed, timber framing tells a story of growth, strength, and the passage of time. With their sculptural curves and natural finishes, straw bale walls become artistic expressions that celebrate the inherent beauty of agricultural byproducts. Off-grid dwellers, through their choice of raw materials, craft homes that resonate with a timeless aesthetic—a blend of tradition and innovation that reflects a profound respect for the intrinsic qualities of the materials themselves.

The adaptability and accessibility of natural materials empower off-grid dwellers to engage in the construction process actively. The techniques associated with building with mud, timber framing, or straw bales are often learnable and conducive to community participation. Off-grid communities foster a spirit of collaboration, where the construction of homes becomes a collective endeavor. Workshops, apprenticeships, and shared knowledge create an atmosphere of continuous learning and skill development, allowing individuals to participate actively in making their living spaces. This hands-on approach builds a sense of ownership and strengthens the social fabric of off-grid communities, creating bonds forged in creating shelter.

Challenges in building with natural materials in off-grid living include code compliance, structural engineering, and local climate conditions. While natural building techniques have a rich history and many success stories, they may encounter regulatory hurdles in some jurisdictions that primarily recognize conventional construction methods. Off-grid dwellers often navigate these challenges by working closely with local authorities and building professionals and incorporating hybrid approaches that combine natural and traditional materials. Structural engineering considerations become crucial, especially in seismic-prone areas, demanding a balance between the desire for raw materials and the imperative for structural stability. Additionally, the adaptability of natural materials to local climate conditions requires careful planning and design to ensure that homes remain resilient and durable over time.

In conclusion, building with natural materials in off-grid living is more than a construction choice—it is a philosophy that embodies sustainability, self-sufficiency, and a deep respect for the environment. From the earthen walls that breathe with the rhythm of the seasons to the timber frames that echo the strength of the forest, off- grid dwellers create homes that are not just shelters but expressions of a way of life. As they navigate the challenges of code compliance, engineering considerations, and local climates, they forge a path that celebrates the inherent beauty and wisdom of building with materials that connect human habitation with the natural world. In the dance between mud and timber, straw and clay, off-grid communities craft a built environment that is a testament to the harmonious coexistence of human shelter and the planet that sustains it.

Tiny Homes and Alternative Housing

In the ever-evolving landscape of off-grid living, the home concept takes on a new dimension that champions simplicity, resourcefulness, and a profound connection to the environment. Tiny homes and alternative housing emerge as trailblazers in this revolution, challenging traditional notions of size and space. In the pursuit of sustainability, self-sufficiency, and a lighter ecological footprint, off-grid dwellers embark on a journey to redefine the meaning of home. From the charming intimacy of tiny houses to the innovative designs of earthships and yurts, alternative housing becomes a canvas for creativity, individuality, and a conscious choice for a lifestyle that prioritizes quality over quantity.

Tiny homes, often under 500 square feet, epitomize the ethos of minimalism and efficiency in off-grid living. The movement towards small living responds to the desire for financial freedom, reduced environmental impact, and reevaluating what constitutes a fulfilling life. Off-grid dwellers embracing tiny homes prioritize intentional living, carefully curating their possessions and surroundings to align with their values. The design of small homes reflects a meticulous consideration of space, functionality, and the efficient use of resources. Multifunctional furniture, ingenious storage solutions, and open floor plans create homes that are not just compact but also exude a sense of coziness and warmth.

Alternative housing extends beyond traditional construction, exploring innovative and unconventional designs harmonizing with the natural environment. Earthships, for example, are off-grid homes that integrate passive solar design, recycled materials, and sustainable water and waste management systems. These self-sustaining structures, often built partially underground, exemplify the fusion of eco-friendly principles with architectural ingenuity. Inspired by traditional nomadic dwellings, Yurts bring a touch of mobile living to off-grid communities. Their circular design, portable nature, and efficient use of space create homes that are functional and resonate with a sense of cultural heritage.

The shift towards tiny homes and alternative housing in off-grid living is propelled by a desire to break free from the shackles of excess and consumerism. Off-grid dwellers find liberation in downsizing, shedding the burdens of oversized mortgages, excessive possessions, and the environmental impact of larger homes. The simplicity of tiny homes becomes a canvas for personal expression, where off-grid dwellers infuse their spaces with unique touches, reflecting their individuality and a commitment to a more intentional way of life. The embrace of alternative housing becomes a declaration of independence, a conscious choice to redefine success and happiness on one's terms.

The economic benefits of tiny homes and alternative housing in off-grid living are significant. The reduced cost of construction, coupled with the potential for DIY buildings and salvaged materials, makes these housing options accessible to a broader demographic. Off-grid dwellers often find financial freedom in the minimalism of tiny living, freeing up resources for other pursuits, such as sustainable practices, renewable energy systems, or community initiatives. The affordability of alternative housing aligns with the broader goal of financial autonomy in off-grid living, creating pathways for individuals to build homes that are ecologically responsible and economically viable.

The environmental impact of tiny homes and alternative housing is a cornerstone of their appeal in off-grid living. The smaller footprint of these structures reduces the demand for raw materials, energy-intensive construction processes, and the ecological disruption associated with larger homes. By embracing a minimalist lifestyle, off-grid dwellers contribute to the conservation of natural resources and the preservation of ecosystems. Integrating sustainable practices, such as rainwater harvesting, composting toilets, and renewable energy systems, minimizes the environmental footprint of tiny homes and alternative housing, creating homes that are in harmony with the principles of ecological stewardship.

In community-building, tiny homes and alternative housing foster a sense of camaraderie and shared values. Off-grid communities that embrace alternative housing often find common ground in their commitment to sustainability, self-sufficiency, and a desire for a deeper connection with the natural world. The compact nature of these homes encourages a close-knit and collaborative lifestyle, where residents share resources, skills, and a collective vision for a more intentional way of living. The sense of community becomes an integral part of the off-grid experience, transforming alternative housing into homes and hubs of connection and support.

Challenges in adopting tiny homes and alternative housing in off-grid living include zoning regulations, infrastructure considerations, and the need for community acceptance. Zoning regulations in many areas are designed for conventional housing, posing challenges for those wishing to build or place tiny homes or alternative structures. Off-grid dwellers often navigate these hurdles by engaging with local authorities, advocating for policy changes, and participating in community planning initiatives. Infrastructure considerations, such as access to water, energy, and waste management, demand innovative solutions to ensure that alternative housing remains self-sustaining. Accepting tiny homes and alternative housing within communities may require a shift in cultural norms and a deeper understanding of their benefits, individually and collectively.

In conclusion, embracing tiny homes and alternative housing in off-grid living is a testament to the transformative power of intentional choices. From the charming simplicity of tiny houses to the innovative designs of earthships and yurts, off-grid dwellers redefine the meaning of home as they prioritize quality over quantity. In the dance between financial freedom and environmental responsibility, tiny homes become more than just dwellings—they become symbols of liberation and a conscious commitment to a lifestyle that resonates with the principles of sustainability, self-sufficiency, and community. As off-grid communities continue to flourish, the revolution of tiny homes and alternative housing stands as a beacon, guiding the way toward a future where homes are not just shelters but reflections of a life lived with purpose and harmony with the planet.

Insulation and Temperature Regulation

In the intricate dance between human habitation and the natural environment, the mastery of insulation and temperature regulation becomes a symphony in the realm of off-grid living. The pursuit of self-sufficiency, sustainability, and harmony with the surroundings demands a thoughtful approach to maintaining comfortable indoor temperatures while minimizing the reliance on external energy sources. From the choice of building materials to the design of passive heating and cooling systems, off-grid dwellers engage in a delicate choreography to create homes resilient to the extremes of weather. The symphony unfolds as insulation, like a silent maestro, orchestrates a harmonious balance between the inhabitants and the ever-changing elements.

Insulation, often hidden within the walls and roofs of homes, emerges as a silent guardian in the quest for energy efficiency and thermal comfort. In off-grid living, where external energy sources may be limited, insulation becomes a linchpin in reducing heat transfer and regulating indoor temperatures. The choice of insulation materials, their placement, and the overall design of the building envelope become critical considerations in creating a habitat that remains cool in the searing heat of summer and warm in the biting cold of winter.

Natural materials, such as straw bales, cellulose, and wool, stand out as insulation champions in off-grid construction. These materials provide excellent thermal resistance and align with the principles of sustainability and responsible resource use. Straw bale construction, for example, utilizes the inherent insulating properties of straw to create walls that offer exceptional temperature regulation. The thick walls of straw-bale homes act as natural buffers, slowing the transfer of heat and cold and creating comfortable and stable interiors. The integration of raw insulation materials manifests the off-grid ethos, where every element of the home contributes to the overall goal of resilience and self-sufficiency.

Passive design principles further enhance the thermal performance of off-grid homes, using the natural elements to regulate indoor temperatures. The strategic placement of windows, orientation of the building, and consideration of local climate conditions become integral aspects of passive design. Off-grid dwellers maximize solar gain in cold climates by positioning windows to capture the low winter sun. In contrast, they employ shading devices and reflective materials to minimize direct sunlight in hot climates. The synergy between insulation and passive design creates homes that dance with the rhythms of the seasons, responding dynamically to the temperature nuances of their specific location.

Incorporating thermal mass adds another layer to the symphony of temperature regulation in off-grid living. Materials with high thermal mass, such as adobe, rammed earth, or even water containers, act as heat sinks, absorbing excess heat during the day and releasing it at night. This natural process of thermal inertia helps stabilize indoor temperatures, preventing rapid fluctuations and reducing the need for external heating or cooling systems. Off-grid dwellers, attuned to passive design and thermal mass principles, create homes that breathe with the natural ebb and flow of temperature, fostering a comfortable and energy-efficient living environment.

Challenges in insulation and temperature regulation in off-grid living include the variability of climate conditions, adaptability, and energy efficiency considerations. Off-grid dwellers often navigate diverse climates, from scorching deserts to chilly mountain landscapes, demanding a flexible approach to insulation strategies. The adaptability of insulation materials and design becomes crucial, allowing homes to respond to the specific challenges presented by each environment. Additionally, while insulation is critical in reducing the need for external heating and cooling, off-grid dwellers must balance comfort with energy efficiency, exploring innovative technologies and alternative energy sources to maintain a sustainable and self-sufficient lifestyle.

In the context of energy efficiency, integrating renewable energy systems becomes a complementary melody in the thermal symphony of off-grid living. Solar panels, wind turbines, and hydropower systems offer a decentralized and sustainable energy source for heating, cooling, and other household needs. The synergy between effective insulation and renewable energy systems amplifies the overall efficiency of off-grid homes, creating a harmonious blend of passive design, natural materials, and clean energy. By embracing this holistic approach, off-grid dwellers reduce their environmental impact and cultivate a lifestyle that aligns with the principles of resilience and ecological responsibility.

The economic considerations of insulation and temperature regulation in off-grid living extend beyond the initial investment in materials and design. While the upfront costs of high-quality insulation and passive design features may constitute a significant expense, the long-term savings on energy bills and maintenance contribute to the financial sustainability of off-grid homes. The integration of renewable energy systems further reinforced the economic viability of off-grid living, offering a pathway to energy independence and reduced reliance on external utilities. The economic benefits of adequate insulation and temperature regulation resonate with the broader goal of financial autonomy, allowing off-grid dwellers to invest in the durability and longevity of their homes.

From an environmental perspective, mastering insulation and temperature regulation in off-grid living aligns with the urgent need for climate-conscious practices. Reducing energy consumption, reliance on sustainable materials, and integrating renewable energy systems contribute to a lifestyle that treads lightly on the planet. By creating homes that are resilient to climate extremes, off-grid dwellers minimize their carbon footprint and make a tangible contribution to the global efforts to combat climate change. The thermal symphony of off-grid living becomes a small yet impactful refrain in the larger chorus of sustainable living practices.

The journey into insulation and temperature regulation in off-grid living is not just a technical pursuit but a holistic exploration of the relationship between human habitation and the natural world.

As off-grid dwellers choose materials that echo the whispers of sustainability, design homes that dance with the rhythms of the seasons, and integrate renewable energy systems that harness the power of nature, they embark on a journey that transcends the boundaries of shelter. In the thermal symphony of off-grid living, insulation becomes the conductor, orchestrating a harmonious balance between comfort and conservation, resilience and resourcefulness. As the melody unfolds, off-grid dwellers create homes that shelter and contribute to a future where every note is played in harmony with the planet.

CHAPTER VI

Growing Your Own Food

Organic Gardening Techniques

In the vibrant tapestry of off-grid living, where self-sufficiency and sustainability weave the fabric of daily life, organic gardening is a cornerstone—a celebration of the profound connection between individuals and the land they inhabit. As off-grid dwellers embrace a lifestyle that prioritizes harmony with nature, cultivating food through organic gardening becomes a practical necessity and a joyful and regenerative endeavor. From the careful selection of seeds to the implementation of permaculture principles, the world of organic gardening unfolds as an art and science, inviting off-grid communities to dance with the seasons, the soil, and life cycles.

At the heart of organic gardening lies the commitment to cultivating food in harmony with nature, eschewing synthetic chemicals, and embracing sustainable practices. Off-grid dwellers, often residing in ecologically sensitive areas, become stewards of the land, nurturing soil health and biodiversity through organic gardening techniques. Using organic fertilizers, compost, and cover crops becomes a conscious choice to replenish the soil with nutrients, fostering a regenerative cycle that mimics the resilience of natural ecosystems. In the dance between the gardener and the soil, organic gardening becomes a dialogue, a partnership where both parties contribute to the flourishing of life.

Companion planting, a practice rooted in traditional wisdom, becomes a strategic element of organic gardening in off-grid living. By selecting plant combinations that complement each other in terms of growth patterns, pest resistance, and nutrient uptake, off-grid dwellers create synergistic relationships within the garden. The interplay between companion plants enhances biodiversity and acts as a natural pest control mechanism, reducing the need for chemical interventions. The artful arrangement of diverse plant species becomes a canvas of resilience, where each plant supports the overall health and balance of the garden ecosystem.

Permaculture, a design philosophy that mirrors the patterns and relationships in natural ecosystems, guides the layout and structure of off-grid gardens. Organic gardening in permaculture embraces diversity, observation, and integration principles. Off-grid dwellers design gardens that mimic the efficiency and resilience of natural ecosystems, utilizing guilds—plant combinations that mutually benefit each other—to create self-sustaining microcosms. The integration of fruit trees, nitrogen-fixing plants, and ground covers exemplifies the permaculture approach, creating gardens that yield abundant harvests and contribute to the overall health of the environment.

Water management in organic gardening becomes a delicate dance between conservation and efficiency. Off-grid dwellers, often reliant on rainwater harvesting and limited water sources, employ mulching, swales, and drip irrigation strategies to optimize water use. Mulching, with materials such as straw or wood chips, retains soil moisture, suppresses weeds, and adds organic matter to the soil. Swales, strategically designed ditches on contour, capture and direct rainwater to where it is needed most, preventing erosion and promoting infiltration. Drip irrigation systems deliver water directly to the root zones of plants, minimizing wastage and maximizing efficiency. In the arid landscapes where off-grid living often takes root, the art of water-wise organic gardening becomes a testament to the ingenuity and resourcefulness of those who cultivate life in harmony with the environment.

Seed saving, an age-old practice that transcends generations, has become vital to organic gardening in off-grid communities. By selecting and preserving seeds from robust and resilient plants, off-grid dwellers create a lineage of varieties adapted to their specific microclimates. Seed saving fosters biodiversity and empowers communities with a sense of self-reliance and resilience. The exchange of seeds within off-grid networks becomes a celebration of diversity, as each seed carries the potential to unlock a tapestry of flavors, textures, and adaptations. In the dance of seasons, seed saving becomes a timeless ritual—a gesture of reciprocity with the earth that sustains and nourishes.

Composting, the alchemical process of transforming kitchen scraps and garden waste into nutrient-rich humus, has become the heartbeat of organic gardening in off-grid living. Compost, often called "black gold," enriches the soil with essential nutrients, improves structure, and enhances water retention. Off-grid dwellers embrace composting toilets to close the loop on nutrient cycles, turning human waste into valuable compost for the garden. The integration of composting in off-grid living reduces reliance on external inputs. It transforms waste into a valuable resource, closing the loop in a regenerative cycle that mirrors the cycles of nature.

Challenges in organic gardening in off-grid living include adapting to local climates, mitigating pest pressures, and balancing productivity with sustainability. Off-grid dwellers often navigate diverse and sometimes harsh climates, requiring a nuanced understanding of regional growing conditions and microclimates. Strategies such as microclimatic design, shade structures, and season extension techniques become tools in the organic gardener's toolkit. Pest pressures, while mitigated through companion planting and natural predators, demand a vigilant approach to observation and intervention. Off-grid communities engage in integrated pest management, utilizing organic solutions and fostering a balance between pests and beneficial insects. Balancing the productivity of gardens with sustainability principles involves thoughtful consideration of resource use, land management, and the long-term health of the ecosystem. Off-grid dwellers, attuned to the delicate dance with nature, navigate these challenges with a commitment to regenerative practices that honor both the immediate needs of sustenance and the enduring health of the environment.

In conclusion, organic gardening in off-grid living transcends the act of cultivating food—it becomes a profound expression of a lifestyle that harmonizes with nature. From carefully selecting seeds to integrating permaculture principles, off-grid dwellers engage in an artful and scientific exploration of cultivating abundance. Organic gardening becomes a dance, a dialogue, and a celebration of the interconnectedness between humans and the land they call home. As off-grid communities cultivate life in harmony with the environment, organic gardening is a testament to the regenerative power of individuals and communities working in partnership with the earth.

Permaculture Principles

In the intricate dance between human habitation and the natural world, permaculture principles emerge as a guiding philosophy, offering a blueprint for designing sustainable, resilient, and regenerative systems. Rooted in the vision of coexisting with nature, permaculture transcends gardening or farming—it becomes a way of life, a holistic approach to creating harmonious and autonomous environments. In the context of off-grid living, where the rhythms of the land and the need for self-sufficiency converge, permaculture principles stand as beacons, illuminating a path that embraces diversity, cycles, and thoughtful design.

At its core, permaculture embodies the ethos of observing and interacting with the natural environment. In the context of off-grid living, this principle becomes a foundational step—a call to keenly observe the landscape's patterns, processes, and relationships. Off- grid dwellers dialogue with the land, studying its contours, microclimates, and ecological niches. Through this intimate observation, they gain insights that inform thoughtful decisions in design and implementation. Observing becomes a bridge, connecting off-grid communities with the inherent wisdom of the natural world.

Designing with nature, not against it, is a fundamental tenet of permaculture principles. Off-grid dwellers, in pursuing sustainable living, emulate the efficiency and resilience found in natural ecosystems. This emulation takes shape through permaculture designs integrating diverse elements to create functional and regenerative landscapes. From food forests that mimic the layers of a natural forest to swales that capture and channel water as rivers do in the landscape, permaculture designs become living systems that thrive on cooperation rather than competition. The essence of this principle lies in the recognition that the land, when treated as a partner rather than a resource, responds with abundance and balance.

In off-grid permaculture, obtaining a yield while ensuring long-term sustainability becomes a delicate balance—a dance with the seasons and the cycles of life. Permaculture designs are conceived not just for immediate harvests but with a foresight that nurtures the health of the land over the years. Food production, water management, and energy harvesting are orchestrated in a way that provides for the community's immediate needs while also investing in the enduring fertility and resilience of the ecosystem. This principle embodies a profound understanding that obtaining a yield is not a one-time transaction but an ongoing relationship with the land.

Applying the principle of self-regulation and feedback in off-grid permaculture involves recognizing that systems are dynamic and subject to change. Off-grid dwellers embrace the concept of feedback loops, where the outcomes of their actions inform future decisions. For example, observing how water flows through the landscape during a rainstorm might prompt swale adjustments or the placement of water catchment systems. The principle of self-regulation acknowledges that off-grid systems are not static; they evolve, adapt, and respond to the changing conditions of the environment. This dynamic responsiveness becomes a critical element of the resilience of permaculture designs.

Energy efficiency, a core tenet of permaculture, becomes a guiding principle in off-grid living. Off-grid dwellers harness and utilize energy with mindfulness to minimize waste and maximize efficiency. Passive solar design, for instance, capitalizes on the natural movements of the sun to regulate indoor temperatures, reducing the need for external heating and cooling systems. Renewable energy systems, such as solar panels or wind turbines, align with the permaculture principle of capturing and storing energy for future use. By integrating energy-efficient practices, off-grid communities cultivate a lifestyle that aligns with the principles of sustainability and self-sufficiency.

The principle of integration in permaculture invites off-grid dwellers to connect the dots between different elements within their living systems. Integration fosters relationships between plants, animals, structures, and water management systems, creating a web of interconnected functions. For example, integrating chickens into a garden serves multiple purposes—they provide pest control, contribute to soil fertility through droppings, and offer a potential source of eggs or meat. The essence of integration lies in recognizing the synergy between elements, where each component serves multiple functions, contributing to the overall health and productivity of the system.

In off-grid permaculture, the principle of small-scale, intensive systems becomes a pragmatic approach to maximizing efficiency and productivity. Off-grid dwellers often work with limited space and resources, prompting them to focus on high-yield, low-maintenance systems. Small-scale gardens, raised beds, or vertical growing structures exemplify this principle, allowing for close management, easy maintenance, and efficient use of resources. The emphasis on small-scale, intensive systems aligns with the idea that every square foot of land and every drop of water can be optimized for productive use in off-grid living.

The principle of using and valuing diversity in off-grid permaculture recognizes that diversity fosters resilience. In the design of food systems, incorporating a variety of plant species provides a range of flavors and nutrients and mitigates the risk of crop failure due to pests or diseases. Biodiversity in off-grid permaculture extends beyond plant species to include animals, insects, and microorganisms. This celebration of diversity reflects an understanding that resilient systems thrive on the richness of interactions among many elements.

The principle of using edges and valuing the marginal in off-grid permaculture acknowledges that the most productive and dynamic areas often occur at the intersections of different environments. Off-grid dwellers capitalize on edges—whether the meeting of a meadow and a forest or the border between a pond and dry land. These transitional zones are rich in diversity and productivity, offering opportunities for creative design and abundant yields. Valuing the marginal also extends to using overlooked or underutilized resources, turning what might be considered waste into valuable inputs for the system.

The principle of creatively using and responding to change in off-grid permaculture invites adaptability and innovation. Off-grid dwellers recognize that change is inevitable in climate patterns, soil conditions, or community dynamics. This principle encourages an openness to evolving strategies and practices in response to changing circumstances. It fosters a mindset of continuous learning and adaptation, embracing the ebb and flow of life in off-grid living.

In conclusion, permaculture principles in off-grid living transcend the realm of agricultural practices—they become a philosophy, a way of engaging with the land and the community. From keen observation and thoughtful design to embracing diversity and responding to change, permaculture principles offer a compass for navigating the complexities of sustainable living. In the dance between the observer and the observed, the designer and the design, off-grid communities embody the essence of permaculture—a harmonious and regenerative relationship with the natural world. As the principles take root in the daily practices of off-grid dwellers, they become guidelines and a celebration of a lifestyle that cultivates resilience, abundance, and harmony with the earth.

Raising Livestock in an Eco-Friendly Manner

In the tapestry of sustainable and off-grid living, the harmonious integration of livestock becomes a pivotal thread, weaving together the interconnected relationships between humans, animals, and the land. The endeavor to raise livestock in an eco-friendly manner transcends the conventional model of industrial farming, where large-scale operations often contribute to environmental degradation. In off-grid living, where self- sufficiency and ecological balance are paramount, a symbiotic dance with livestock unfolds—a dance that honors the welfare of animals regenerates the land and nurtures a holistic approach to agriculture.

Ethical and eco-friendly livestock management principles begin with the recognition that animals are integral partners in the intricate choreography of off-grid ecosystems. Unlike the confined spaces of factory farms, where animals are treated as mere commodities, off-grid dwellers embrace a model that prioritizes the well-being of livestock. In this dance with nature, animals are not just producers of meat, milk, or wool; they become stewards of the land, contributing to soil fertility, weed control, and overall ecosystem health. The ethos of ethical livestock management is rooted in the understanding that animals are sentient beings with a role to play in the cyclical rhythms of life.

Pasture-based systems are a cornerstone in eco-friendly livestock management, allowing animals to express their natural behaviors while regenerating the land. Off-grid dwellers design rotational grazing systems that mimic the migratory patterns of wild herbivores, allowing livestock to graze in one area before moving to fresh pasture. This approach prevents overgrazing, encourages plant diversity, and supports the natural nutrient cycling of the ecosystem. By harnessing the innate behaviors of animals and aligning them with the rhythms of the land, pasture-based systems become a testament to the harmony that can be achieved in the dance between livestock and the environment.

Regenerative agriculture, a guiding principle in eco-friendly livestock management, sees animals not as problems to be solved but as partners in soil health and fertility. Integrating livestock into rotational systems creates a symbiotic relationship where animals graze, deposit organic matter, and stimulate the growth of pasture plants. The natural interactions between animals and the land result in enhanced soil structure, increased water retention, and the sequestration of carbon—a regenerative dance that heals the earth rather than depletes it. Off-grid dwellers embrace this principle, recognizing that livestock can be catalysts for positive change in the soil's health and the ecosystem's vitality.

In eco-friendly livestock management, the holistic health of animals takes precedence over the narrow pursuit of maximizing production. Off-grid dwellers prioritize natural and humane treatment, providing animals access to clean water, ample space, and a diet that aligns with their physiological needs. In contrast to the routine use of antibiotics and growth hormones in industrial farming, eco-friendly practices emphasize preventive healthcare and natural remedies. Animals become partners in the dance of life, exhibiting behaviors that reflect their contentment and well-being. The principles of holistic health extend beyond physical care to include mental and emotional aspects, recognizing that a stress-free and enriched environment contributes to the overall welfare of livestock.

Diversified livestock systems, where different species complement each other, become a hallmark of eco-friendly management in off-grid living. Polyculture, the intentional mixing of species, mirrors the diversity found in natural ecosystems. For example, chickens scratching and pecking in the vicinity of larger livestock control pests and spread manure, fostering a nutrient-rich environment. With their affinity for water, ducks can be integrated into aquaponic systems, contributing to nutrient cycling and pest control. The dance of diversified livestock systems enhances resilience, reduces the reliance on external inputs, and fosters a dynamic and self-sustaining agricultural landscape.

Integrating animals in agroforestry, another facet of eco-friendly livestock management, blurs the boundaries between traditional farming and forestry. Silvopasture systems, where livestock graze among trees, offer multiple benefits. The shade trees mitigate heat stress in animals, while their presence contributes to increased biodiversity and carbon sequestration. The integration of livestock in agroforestry not only enhances the ecological functions of the land but also diversifies income streams for off-grid dwellers. This dance with agroforestry represents a departure from monoculture practices, reflecting an understanding that a harmonious balance between animals and trees can yield economic and ecological rewards.

Water management becomes a critical element in the eco-friendly dance of livestock in off-grid living. Off-grid dwellers employ rainwater harvesting, swales, and contour trenches to capture and manage water for animals and vegetation. By maximizing the efficiency of water use, off-grid communities ensure that livestock have access to clean and sufficient water while also contributing to the overall sustainability of the land. The thoughtful design of water systems becomes an integral part of the dance with livestock, fostering resilience and adaptability in the face of changing environmental conditions.

Eco-friendly livestock management in off-grid living presents challenges such as the requirement for climate adaptation, striking a balance between sustainability and productivity, and handling conflicts with wildlife. Off-grid dwellers often navigate diverse and sometimes challenging climates, demanding an adaptable approach to livestock management. This may involve selecting breeds and species well-suited to local conditions, implementing shelter designs that protect from extreme weather, and incorporating season-specific management practices. Balancing productivity with sustainability requires thoughtful consideration of stocking rates, pasture management, and nutrient cycling to ensure that the land remains healthy and productive in the long term. The potential for conflicts with wildlife, such as predation or competition for resources, necessitates strategies for coexistence and the implementation of protective measures that safeguard both domestic animals and native fauna.

In conclusion, raising livestock in an eco-friendly manner in the context of off-grid living is a dynamic and multifaceted dance that honors the intrinsic value of animals, regenerates the land, and fosters a holistic approach to agriculture. From pasture-based systems and regenerative practices to diversified livestock systems and water management strategies, off-grid dwellers have a harmonious relationship with the environment. In this dance with nature, livestock become partners, contributors, and stewards, embodying the principles of ethical and sustainable living. As the rhythms of the dance unfold, off-grid communities not only nurture the well-being of their animals but also cultivate landscapes that are vibrant, resilient, and in tune with the intricate melodies of the natural world.

CHAPTER VII

Waste Management and Recycling

Zero-Waste Practices

In pursuing sustainable living, off-grid communities champion a revolutionary concept that transcends the traditional norms of resource consumption—the zero-waste lifestyle. At its core, zero-waste practices represent a commitment to minimizing waste generation, redefining consumption patterns, and fostering a profound sense of responsibility for the environmental impact of daily choices in the context of off-grid living, where self- sufficiency and harmony with nature guide every decision, zero-waste practices emerge as a symphony—a harmonious integration of mindful consumption, resourcefulness, and ecological stewardship.

At the heart of the zero-waste movement is refusing unnecessary consumption. Off-grid dwellers adopt a discerning approach to purchases, questioning the necessity of each item and its long-term impact. By refusing single-use plastics, disposable products, and items with excessive packaging, off-grid communities reduce the influx of non-biodegradable waste into their living spaces. This practice extends beyond the immediate benefits of waste reduction—it becomes a mindset shift, encouraging a conscious reevaluation of individual needs and promoting a connection with the intrinsic value of the resources being used.

Zero-waste practices in off-grid living emphasize the importance of reusing and repurposing materials. Items considered waste in conventional settings find new life and purpose in the hands of resourceful off-grid dwellers. Jars become storage containers, old clothing transforms into rags or quilts, and discarded wood finds its place in construction or as fuel. The art of repurposing becomes a creative endeavor, changing the perception of waste from disposable to valuable. In this symphony of resourcefulness, every object is viewed through the lens of potential, inviting a culture of creativity and innovation.

Composting, a cornerstone of zero-waste practices, becomes a regenerative act in off-grid living. Off-grid communities implement composting systems that transform kitchen scraps and organic waste into nutrient-rich soil amendments. Composting not only diverts organic matter from landfills but also enriches the soil, creating a closed-loop system that mirrors the cycles of nature. Off-grid dwellers, attuned to permaculture principles, integrate composting into their agricultural practices, turning waste into a valuable resource that nourishes the land and supports food cultivation.

In the orchestration of a zero-waste lifestyle, recycling becomes a deliberate and strategic action. Off-grid communities prioritize easily recyclable materials, opting for glass, metal, and paper over plastics with limited recycling potential. Without municipal recycling services, off-grid dwellers often develop creative solutions, such as establishing community recycling centers or collaborating with nearby facilities. Recycling, in the context of zero-waste practices, is not a passive act but an intentional choice that reflects a commitment to minimizing the environmental footprint.

The concept of precycling, an extension of zero-waste principles, emphasizes the reduction of waste at the source. Off-grid dwellers make mindful choices during purchasing, opting for products with minimal packaging or choosing items in bulk to reduce overall packaging waste. Precycling involves considering the life cycle of a product before it enters the home, prompting off-grid communities to favor products with environmentally friendly packaging or, ideally, no packaging at all. The practice of precycling reflects a holistic understanding that waste reduction begins not at the disposal stage but at the point of acquisition.

In the dance of zero-waste living, energy efficiency becomes intertwined with waste reduction. Off-grid communities embrace energy-efficient appliances, harness renewable energy sources, and prioritize energy conservation practices. The correlation between energy use and waste production is acknowledged, as the extraction, production, and disposal of goods contribute to carbon emissions and environmental degradation. Off-grid dwellers, by aligning zero-waste practices with energy efficiency, cultivate a lifestyle that harmonizes with sustainability principles, recognizing that waste reduction is an environmental responsibility and an energy-conscious choice.

Water conservation emerges as a crucial component of zero-waste practices in off-grid living. Off-grid dwellers, often reliant on rainwater harvesting or limited water sources, implement strategies to minimize water waste. Low-flow fixtures, greywater recycling systems, and mindful water usage have become integral to the zero-waste lifestyle. The understanding that water is a finite and precious resource prompts off-grid communities to approach water consumption with reverence and responsibility. In the symphony of zero-waste living, water conservation harmonizes with waste reduction, creating a holistic approach that reflects an interconnected understanding of resource stewardship.

Adapting to local conditions, considering off-grid energy limits, and the scarcity of recycling facilities are some challenges associated with zero-waste living off the grid. Off-grid dwellers often need help with the absence of nearby recycling centers, requiring them to devise innovative solutions such as creating communal recycling hubs or collaborating with neighboring communities. The adaptability of zero-waste practices to diverse local conditions, from arid landscapes to forested areas, demands a flexible approach that considers the specific challenges and opportunities each environment presents. Additionally, the integration of zero-waste practices must align with the energy constraints of off-grid living, as the recycling and processing of materials may require energy-intensive processes. Off-grid communities navigate these challenges with ingenuity, resourcefulness, and a commitment to continuous improvement.

In conclusion, the symphony of zero-waste practices in off-grid living is multifaceted. This deliberate dance resonates with sustainability, mindfulness, and ecological stewardship. From refusing unnecessary consumption to embracing the regenerative power of composting, off-grid dwellers embody a lifestyle that aspires to generate minimal waste and leave a positive imprint on the planet. As the principles of zero-waste living become woven into the fabric of daily life, off-grid communities reduce their environmental impact and contribute to a global movement towards a more sustainable and harmonious existence. In this symphony, every action becomes a note, every choice a melody, and every individual a participant in the rhythmic dance of a zero-waste lifestyle.

Creative Upcycling Projects

In off-grid living, where self-sufficiency and sustainability converge, creative upcycling projects are a testament to the artful fusion of ingenuity and ecological responsibility. Beyond the conventional notions of recycling, upcycling elevates discarded materials to new heights, transforming them into functional, artistic, and often whimsical creations. The ethos of upcycling resonates deeply with off-grid dwellers, for whom resourcefulness and a commitment to minimizing waste are fundamental principles. In this world where necessity sparks invention, creative upcycling projects become a vibrant tapestry—a celebration of innovation, environmental consciousness, and the beauty that can arise from the most unexpected sources.

At its essence, upcycling represents a departure from the linear model of consumption and disposal. Instead of viewing items as single-use or disposable, off-grid communities embrace a circular approach that breathes new life into discarded materials. Old wooden pallets, disused shipping containers, discarded windows, and retired car tires become the raw materials for creative upcycling projects. The transformation begins not in manufacturing plants but in the minds and hands of individuals who see potential where others see waste. This shift in perspective becomes the catalyst for a cascade of artistic endeavors, from functional furniture crafted from reclaimed wood to cozy shelters fashioned from repurposed shipping containers.

In creative upcycling, discarded furniture takes on a new lease of life. Old wooden doors become elegant dining tables, discarded pallets morph into stylish outdoor seating, and retired industrial drums transform into quirky coffee tables. The artistry lies not just in the aesthetics but in the story embedded within each piece— an ode to its previous life and a testament to the vision of its creator. Off-grid dwellers, often residing in remote areas with limited access to conventional furniture stores, harness the power of upcycling to furnish their homes with unique, handmade creations that carry the imprint of nature and human ingenuity.

Architectural upcycling becomes a hallmark of off-grid construction, where innovative structures rise from unconventional materials. Once relegated to the sidelines of shipping yards, shipping containers become the building blocks for off-grid homes. The modular and robust nature of containers lends itself to efficient and sustainable construction, offering a solution to the challenges of remote living. Discarded windows, salvaged from renovation projects or demolition sites, find new purpose in creating greenhouse structures, capturing sunlight, and extending growing seasons for off-grid gardens. The architecture of upcycling becomes a fusion of functionality, aesthetics, and environmental consciousness—a dance between form and purpose.

Creative upcycling projects extend beyond the utilitarian to the realm of artistic expression. Off-grid communities embrace the challenge of transforming discarded materials into sculptures, murals, and installations that grace the landscape. Rusty Farm implements metamorphosis into kinetic wind sculptures, abandoned driftwood is woven into intricate outdoor art installations, and discarded metal scraps are welded into avant-garde sculptures. The art of upcycling transcends the boundaries of traditional art forms, inviting off-grid dwellers to become both creators and curators of their outdoor galleries—a testament to the transformative power of imagination and resourcefulness.

In the dance of creative upcycling, off-grid gardens become canvases for repurposed artistry. Discarded tires find new purpose as planters, transforming mundane rubber into vibrant, cascading displays of flowers. Pallets become vertical gardens, breathing life into walls and fences with herbs, flowers, and succulents. The integration of upcycled art in off-grid gardens adds a touch of whimsy and embodies the principles of sustainability, reimagining the potential of everyday materials in creating outdoor sanctuaries.

The world of fashion in off-grid living embraces the ethos of upcycling, turning old garments and textiles into new and fashionable attire. Discarded denim jeans find new life as stylish bags, worn-out t-shirts become trendy scarves, and vintage fabrics are repurposed into eclectic clothing. Off-grid dwellers, often distant from mainstream fashion trends, cultivate a unique and sustainable style through the art of upcycling. Transforming old clothes into new fashion pieces becomes a personal and creative expression, reflecting the individuality and resourcefulness of those who embrace a lifestyle that prioritizes style and sustainability.

Creative upcycling projects extend their influence to practicality, with repurposed tools and implements finding new roles in off-grid life. Old barrels become rainwater harvesting systems, retired wheel rims are repurposed as fire pits, and discarded wine bottles transform into solar-powered lanterns. The ingenuity lies in repurposing and the seamless integration of functionality and aesthetics. Off-grid dwellers, often resourceful by necessity, turn to upcycling to optimize the utility of available materials while minimizing waste. This practical dance resonates with the principles of self-sufficiency.

The art of upcycling is in the context of off-grid living. Off-grid dwellers navigate the limitations of available materials, balancing creativity with practicality. The remote locations of many off-grid communities pose logistical challenges, requiring resourcefulness in sourcing discarded materials. The harsh conditions of some off-grid environments, whether extreme temperatures or inclement weather, demand durability and resilience in upcycled creations. Additionally, the scarcity of specialized tools and equipment in off-grid settings prompts the development of innovative and low-tech solutions to execute creative upcycling projects. Despite these challenges, the spirit of ingenuity prevails as off-grid communities find joy and fulfillment in transforming cast-offs into cherished creations.

In conclusion, creative upcycling projects in off-grid living epitomize the symbiotic relationship between human ingenuity and ecological responsibility. From repurposed furniture and architectural innovations to artistic expressions and practical tools, the dance of upcycling weaves a narrative of resourcefulness, sustainability, and the celebration of discarded materials. In the hands of off-grid dwellers, upcycling becomes not just a means of waste reduction but a profound expression of a lifestyle that values creativity, self-sufficiency, and a harmonious coexistence with the environment. As discarded materials find new purpose and stories unfold in the transformation process, creative upcycling becomes a vibrant and evolving symphony—a testament to the beauty that arises when human creativity dances in harmony with the rhythms of nature.

Composting for a Healthy Garden

In the realm of sustainable and off-grid living, the practice of composting stands as a cornerstone. This transformative alchemy turns kitchen scraps, yard waste, and organic debris into a nutrient-rich elixir for the garden. The essence of composting goes beyond the mere disposal of garbage; it embodies a profound relationship between humans and the Earth, where the cycles of decay and renewal become a dance of regeneration. In the context of off-grid living, where self-sufficiency and harmony with nature prevail, composting becomes not just a gardening technique but a holistic philosophy— nurturing the soil, fostering biodiversity, and creating a closed-loop system that mirrors the cycles of life.

Composting is a biological process driven by the intricate interactions of microorganisms, fungi, and microorganisms. Off-grid communities harness the power of decomposition to break down organic matter, transforming it into a nutrient-dense material that enhances soil structure, fertility, and water retention. Kitchen scraps, such as vegetable peels, coffee grounds, and eggshells, join forces with yard waste like leaves, grass clippings, and prunings to form the raw ingredients for this natural alchemy. The compost pile becomes a microcosm of life, teeming with bacteria that initiate the decomposition process, fungi that break down complex organic compounds, and macroorganisms like worms and insects that aerate and mix the pile.

In off-grid gardens, composting goes beyond the conventional bin or pile—it becomes an integrated and intentional practice woven into the fabric of sustainable agriculture. Off-grid dwellers design composting systems that align with permaculture principles, integrating composting into garden beds, orchards, and food forests.

This intentional placement allows the nutrients generated through composting to nourish the plants, creating a regenerative cycle where waste becomes a valuable resource. Composting in off-grid gardens is not just a means of waste reduction but a dynamic and reciprocal relationship between the gardener and the soil.

The capacity of composting to enhance soil structure is one of its main advantages. In off-grid environments, where access to external inputs may be limited, healthy and fertile soil development becomes paramount. Compost acts as a soil conditioner, enhancing its texture, water-holding capacity, and drainage. The organic matter in compost binds with soil particles, creating aggregates for better aeration and root penetration. In the dance of composting, the soil becomes a living entity rich with the microbial life that sustains plant health and vitality.

Composting becomes a vital tool for off-grid communities to address soil fertility challenges. Without synthetic fertilizers, off-grid gardeners rely on compost to supply essential nutrients to plants. The nutrient content of compost varies depending on the mix of materials, with nitrogen-rich kitchen scraps balancing carbon-rich yard waste. This diversity of inputs ensures that compost provides a broad spectrum of nutrients, fostering a balanced and resilient ecosystem in the soil. Off-grid dwellers, attuned to sustainable agriculture principles, view compost not just as a means of plant nutrition but as a holistic approach to building a fertile and self-sustaining environment.

Water conservation becomes an inherent benefit of composting in off-grid gardens. The organic matter in compost acts as a sponge, enhancing the soil's water-holding capacity and reducing the need for frequent irrigation. In arid or off-grid environments where water resources are precious, composting becomes a strategy for maximizing water use efficiency. The dance of composting, with its ability to create soil that retains moisture, aligns seamlessly with sustainability principles, fostering a garden that thrives with minimal water input.

The biodiversity that thrives in compost piles contributes to pest and disease management in off-grid gardens. Beneficial microorganisms and macroorganisms, including predatory insects and nematodes, establish a delicate balance that helps control harmful pests and pathogens. Off-grid dwellers, recognizing the interconnected web of life in the garden, view composting as a holistic practice that nourishes plants and fosters a resilient and biodiverse ecosystem. In this dance between the compost pile and the garden, the principles of permaculture and ecological harmony come to life.

Composting becomes a powerful strategy for off-grid waste management, turning what might be considered garbage into a valuable resource. Without municipal waste services, off-grid communities rely on composting to divert organic matter from landfills and create a closed- loop system. Kitchen scraps, garden clippings, and other organic waste return to the soil, completing the cycle of life. Composting becomes a tangible expression of the off-grid ethos—a commitment to responsible and sustainable living that extends beyond the garden's boundaries.

In the context of off-grid living, composting requires a nuanced approach considering the specific challenges and opportunities of remote or rural environments. Off-grid dwellers often need help with the types of materials available for composting, necessitating adaptability and resourcefulness. For example, the absence of municipal green waste collections may require off-grid communities to explore alternative sources of carbon-rich materials, such as straw, wood chips, or dried leaves. The remoteness of some off-grid locations may also pose challenges in sourcing specific composting aids, such as microbial inoculants or diverse composting organisms. In response to these challenges, off-grid communities often develop localized and innovative solutions, leveraging the resources available in their immediate surroundings.

The dance of composting in off-grid living extends beyond the conventional backyard pile or bin. Off-grid communities often explore various composting techniques, such as vermicomposting (using worms), trench composting, or sheet mulching, to suit their needs and conditions. Vermicomposting, in particular, becomes a favored method for off-grid dwellers, as it provides a way to compost kitchen scraps in a confined space while producing nutrient-rich worm castings. The versatility and adaptability of composting techniques in off-grid living reflect a commitment to sustainable practices that harmonize with the unique challenges and opportunities presented by remote or self-sufficient lifestyles.

In conclusion, composting in off-grid living becomes more than a gardening technique—it is a dynamic and regenerative dance that embodies the principles of sustainability, soil health, and waste reduction. The compost pile becomes a microcosm of life, teeming with microbial activity and the alchemy of decay and transformation. In the hands of off-grid dwellers, composting becomes a sacred act—an intentional and reciprocal relationship with the Earth that nourishes the soil and the soul. As kitchen scraps and yard waste metamorphose into black gold for the garden, the dance of composting unfolds as a celebration of life cycles, biodiversity, and the interconnected rhythms of the natural world.

CHAPTER VIII

Smart Technology in Off-Grid Living

Energy-Efficient Appliances

In the enchanting world of off-grid living, where self-sufficiency and environmental consciousness converge, the choice of energy-efficient appliances becomes a harmonious dance—a celebration of innovation, resourcefulness, and a commitment to minimizing one's ecological footprint. Without traditional utility grids, off-grid dwellers navigate a delicate balance between meeting their energy needs and embracing a lifestyle that treads lightly on the planet. Energy-efficient appliances emerge as pivotal players in this intricate dance, offering functionality and a pathway to a sustainable and off-grid existence that resonates with efficiency, conservation, and conscious living principles.

The heartbeat of off-grid living is intimately tied to the efficient use of energy resources. In this dance, energy-efficient appliances take center stage, embodying a commitment to optimizing energy consumption without sacrificing performance. Off-grid communities, often powered by renewable sources such as solar panels or wind turbines, recognize the importance of minimizing energy demand to align with the intermittent nature of these sources. Energy-efficient appliances, designed to operate with minimal energy input, become essential partners in this dance of resourceful living.

Lighting, a fundamental aspect of daily life, undergoes a transformative shift in off-grid living. With their superior energy efficiency and longevity, energy-efficient LED bulbs illuminate homes and spaces, replacing traditional incandescent or halogen counterparts. Off-grid dwellers embrace the warm glow of LED lighting for its efficiency and the extended hours of operation it affords, optimizing the use of the energy stored in batteries or generated by renewable sources. The dance of LED lighting in off-grid living represents a departure from energy-intensive illumination, guiding communities towards a future where efficiency and ambiance coalesce.

In off-grid kitchens, the choreography of energy-efficient appliances unfolds with grace—solar-powered refrigerators, designed with advanced insulation and energy-efficient compressors, cool perishables while minimizing energy consumption. Induction cooktops, known for their precision and rapid heating, replace traditional stovetops, offering a culinary dance that balances performance and energy efficiency. Off-grid communities leverage propane-powered ovens and stoves for their efficiency in cooking without the need for extensive electricity, showcasing a nuanced approach that aligns appliance choices with available energy sources.

The dance of energy-efficient appliances extends beyond the confines of indoor spaces to the realm of off-grid heating and cooling. Off-grid dwellers, often residing in diverse climates, embrace energy-efficient solutions that mitigate extreme temperatures without overtaxing energy systems. Efficient wood-burning stoves provide warmth in colder months, harnessing energy in sustainably harvested firewood. Ventilation strategies, such as passive solar design and natural airflow, enhance cooling in warmer climates, reducing reliance on energy-intensive air conditioning. In this dance of temperature regulation, energy-efficient appliances become partners in creating comfortable and sustainable living environments.

Off-grid living demands a discerning approach to water use, and energy-efficient appliances are pivotal in optimizing water-related tasks. High-efficiency washing machines and dishwashers that use less water while maintaining performance standards become integral to off-grid laundry and dishwashing routines. Low-flow faucets and showerheads equipped with aerators minimize water consumption without compromising functionality. Off-grid dwellers, attuned to the interconnected nature of water and energy, orchestrate a dance where every drop is used judiciously, and appliances become conservation instruments.

The dance of energy-efficient appliances extends

outdoors, shaping the off-grid experience in spaces such as workshops, barns, and tool sheds. Off-grid communities employ solar-powered tools, efficient irrigation systems, and energy-conserving equipment to enhance productivity without straining energy resources. In the vast expanse of off-grid landscapes, where access to traditional power grids is a distant prospect, integrating energy-efficient tools is a testament to the resilience and adaptability of off-grid living.

In the symphony of off-grid living, energy-efficient

appliances embody the principles of sustainability, conservation, and self-sufficiency. The choice of these appliances is not just a matter of functionality; it is a conscious decision to align one's lifestyle with the natural world's rhythms. Off-grid dwellers, in their pursuit of a harmonious existence, seek appliances that resonate with the ethos of responsible living. From lighting the spaces they inhabit to powering the tools they use, energy-efficient appliances become integral to the dance of off-grid living—a dance that values efficiency minimizes waste and cultivates a lifestyle attuned to the delicate balance of the Earth.

Adoption of energy-efficient appliances in off-grid living is

hindered by the cost of the initial investment, the need for compatibility with renewable energy sources, and the appliances' longevity and repairability. Off-grid communities often face budget constraints, making the upfront costs of energy-efficient appliances a significant consideration. However, the long-term savings in energy bills and the reduced environmental impact often outweigh these initial expenses, making energy-efficient choices financially viable over time. Compatibility with renewable energy systems, such as solar or wind, is crucial to ensuring that appliances can operate efficiently with these sources' intermittent and variable nature. Off- grid dwellers also prioritize the durability and repairability of appliances, seeking models that can withstand the rigors of off-grid living and easily maintain or repair with limited resources.

In conclusion, the dance of energy-efficient appliances in off-grid living is a nuanced and deliberate choreography— a celebration of choices that reflect a commitment to sustainability, efficiency, and harmonious coexistence with nature. From lighting the night with LED brilliance to powering the tools that shape off-grid landscapes, energy-efficient appliances become essential partners in the journey toward self-sufficiency. As off-grid dwellers navigate the intricate dance of resourcefulness and environmental consciousness, energy-efficient appliances emerge as tools and integral components of a lifestyle that treads lightly on the Earth. In this dance, every watt saved becomes a step towards a sustainable future— where off-grid living becomes a graceful and enlightened ballet, guided by the energy-efficient choices of those who dance to the rhythms of a regenerative Earth.

Off-Grid Internet Solutions

In the vast expanse of off-grid living, where the embrace of nature meets the desire for self-sufficiency, the challenge of connectivity becomes a defining frontier. As the modern world increasingly relies on the digital realm, off-grid dwellers seek solutions that bridge the gap between a life untethered from traditional utilities and the demands of the interconnected age. The quest for off-grid internet solutions unfolds as a strategic dance—a delicate choreography that balances the need for connectivity with the principles of sustainability, adaptability, and independence.

The dance begins with recognizing that traditional internet infrastructure, reliant on centralized power grids and extensive cabling, often eludes remote off-grid locations. In response, off-grid communities turn to alternative technologies that leverage the power of renewable energy sources and embrace a decentralized approach to connectivity. Solar-powered internet setups, equipped with energy-efficient routers and low-energy- consuming devices, become stalwart companions in the dance of off-grid connectivity. These setups align with the ethos of sustainable living and provide a level of autonomy that resonates with the spirit of off-grid independence.

Satellite internet emerges as a prominent player in the off-grid connectivity dance, offering a lifeline to those in remote locations beyond the reach of traditional broadband services. Off-grid dwellers can establish internet connectivity by tapping into satellite signals without relying on terrestrial infrastructure. While satellite internet may have challenges, such as latency and bandwidth limitations, it becomes a crucial tool for bridging the digital divide in off-grid environments. The dance of satellite internet in off-grid living embodies adaptability—a willingness to embrace innovative solutions that transcend the limitations of physical distance.

Mesh networks, another entrant in the off-grid connectivity dance, showcase the power of community-driven solutions. Each connected device serves as a node in a mesh network, creating a web of interlinked communication. Off-grid communities leverage mesh networks to establish localized internet connectivity, allowing information to hop from node to node until it reaches its destination. This dance of interconnectivity fosters community collaboration and mitigates the challenges posed by rugged terrains or vast distances in off-grid landscapes.

The off-grid connectivity dance also incorporates long-range Wi-Fi technology, extending the reach of internet signals beyond the confines of traditional networks. Off-grid dwellers strategically position high-gain antennas to capture and amplify Wi-Fi signals, enabling internet access from greater distances. This dance of long-range Wi-Fi aligns with the self-sufficiency ethos of off-grid living, as it allows communities to tap into existing networks or establish localized connections without reliance on external providers.

Off-grid dwellers often find themselves at the crossroads of digital connectivity and environmental consciousness, prompting a delicate dance between staying connected and minimizing energy consumption. In response, energy-efficient routers and devices become integral components of the off-grid internet solution dance. These devices are designed to operate with minimal energy input, aligning with the intermittent nature of renewable energy sources such as solar or wind. The dance of energy-efficient internet solutions becomes a harmonious collaboration between staying digitally connected and embracing a lifestyle attuned to sustainability principles.

Challenges in off-grid internet solutions include the initial setup costs, the limitations of available technologies, and considerations for data consumption and privacy. Establishing off-grid internet infrastructure often involves upfront investments in equipment, such as satellite dishes, high-gain antennas, and energy-efficient routers. While these costs may pose initial challenges, the long-term benefits of connectivity and autonomy often outweigh the initial expenses. Additionally, off-grid dwellers navigate the limitations of available technologies, acknowledging that certain remote locations may have restricted access to specific internet solutions. The dance of off-grid internet solutions also involves considerations for data consumption, as limited bandwidth in some remote areas may require communities to adopt practices that optimize internet usage. Privacy concerns, an ever-present challenge in the digital age, prompt off-grid dwellers to explore secure and private internet solutions, ensuring that the dance of connectivity does not compromise individual or community privacy.

In conclusion, the dance of off-grid internet solutions is a nuanced and dynamic choreography—a strategic blending of technology, sustainability, and adaptability. As off-grid dwellers navigate the digital wilderness, they seek connectivity solutions that resonate with the principles of self-sufficiency, environmental consciousness, and community collaboration. From solar-powered setups and satellite internet lifelines to mesh networks and long-range Wi-Fi dances, the quest for off-grid connectivity embodies the spirit of innovation and resilience. In this dance, every connection established triumphs over geographical challenges, and every community-driven solution becomes a step towards a future where off-grid living seamlessly integrates with the interconnected rhythms of the modern world.

Automation for Sustainable Living

In the intricate dance of off-grid living, where the rhythms of nature intertwine with the pursuit of self-sufficiency, the integration of automation emerges as a transformative force. This symphony orchestrates efficiency, conservation, and sustainable practices. As technology evolves, off-grid dwellers embrace the power of automation to streamline daily tasks and elevate their commitment to a lifestyle harmonized with the Earth. The dance of automation in off-grid living unfolds as a nuanced and intentional choreography—a celebration of innovation that redefines the boundaries of sustainable existence.

At the heart of the automation dance lies the quest for energy efficiency. Off-grid communities, often reliant on renewable energy sources such as solar or wind, navigate the delicate balance of meeting their energy needs while respecting the intermittent nature of these resources.

Automated energy management systems have become pivotal players in this dance, regulating electricity consumption to align with the availability of renewable energy. These systems intelligently distribute energy among various appliances, prioritize essential tasks, and optimize energy storage. This choreography not only conserves power but maximizes the utilization of the energy harnessed from nature's bounty.

In sustainable agriculture, the dance of automation transforms the landscape of off-grid farming. Automated irrigation systems, powered by renewable energy, deliver precise amounts of water to crops, optimizing hydration without wasteful excess. Smart sensors embedded in the soil provide real-time data on moisture levels, enabling off-grid farmers to make informed decisions about irrigation schedules. The dance of automated farming extends to precision agriculture, where robotic drones monitor crop health, identify pest infestations, and map the topography of off-grid landscapes. In this choreography, automation becomes a guardian of sustainable agriculture, fostering optimal yields while minimizing environmental impact.

Off-grid homes resonate with the harmonies of automation as energy-efficient and automated appliances take center stage. Smart thermostats, synchronized with renewable energy systems, regulate indoor temperatures based on occupancy patterns and weather conditions. Mechanical lighting systems adjust brightness levels according to natural light, minimizing electricity consumption. The dance of home automation extends to water management, with intelligent faucets and showers optimizing water usage. Off-grid dwellers embrace the potential of these technologies not just for convenience but as allies in the pursuit of sustainability. In this dance, every automated task contributes to the symphony of resourceful living.

Waste management in off-grid communities experiences a transformative dance by integrating automated systems. Innovative composting solutions, equipped with sensors and actuators, optimize the composting process by maintaining ideal conditions for decomposition. Mechanical sorting systems streamline recycling efforts, ensuring that off-grid dwellers can efficiently categorize and process recyclable materials. Waste-to-energy systems, guided by automation, convert organic waste into usable energy, closing the resource utilization loop. In this dance of waste management automation, off-grid communities reduce their environmental footprint and actively contribute to the circular economy.

The dance of automation in off-grid living extends beyond individual homes to embrace community-scale solutions. Microgrids, guided by automation, coordinate the energy production and consumption of entire off-grid communities. These intelligent systems prioritize critical infrastructure, such as medical facilities or communal spaces, during periods of limited energy availability. Automated communication networks enhance community connectivity, allowing off-grid residents to share information about weather patterns, agricultural practices, and energy availability. The dance of community-scale automation manifests shared resilience and collaboration, amplifying the sustainability impact of off-grid living.

Challenges in the integration of automation in off-grid living include initial setup costs, the need for adaptability, and considerations for system maintenance and repair. While automation technologies offer long-term benefits, the upfront investment in smart devices, sensors, and automated systems may pose financial challenges for some off-grid communities. The dance of automation also requires adaptability, as technologies and systems must align with the unique conditions of each off-grid location, from varied climates to diverse agricultural practices. Maintenance and repair become crucial considerations, necessitating the development of local expertise and accessible solutions to ensure the sustained functionality of automated systems in remote off-grid environments.

In conclusion, the dance of automation in off-grid living is a multifaceted and transformative choreography—a celebration of innovation that propels sustainable living into new realms. From energy-efficient home systems and precision agriculture to intelligent waste management solutions and community-scale microgrids, automation becomes an ally in the pursuit of self- sufficiency and environmental harmony. The symphony of automation in off-grid living embodies a commitment to efficiency, conservation, and resilience—a dance where technology and sustainability move in unison. As off-grid dwellers continue to embrace the transformative power of automation, the dance unfolds as a testament to the endless possibilities that arise when innovation and environmental consciousness come together in harmony.

CHAPTER IX

Community Building and Networking

Connecting with Like-Minded Individuals

In the vast expanses of off-grid living, where the hum of nature intertwines with the pulse of self-sufficiency, the significance of connecting with like-minded individuals becomes a cornerstone. This bridge spans the distances between remote homesteads and creates a vibrant community tapestry. The dance of forging connections in off-grid living unfolds as a rich and intentional choreography—a celebration of shared values, mutual support, and the collective wisdom that emerges when individuals with a shared vision come together.

At the heart of this dance lies the recognition that off-grid living, while embodying a desire for solitude and independence, thrives on the strength of community bonds. Off-grid dwellers, scattered across rugged landscapes and secluded retreats, share a common thread of seeking a life in harmony with nature, free from the constraints of traditional utilities. The dance of connecting with like-minded individuals becomes a quest for camaraderie, a shared understanding that transcends the challenges and joys of off-grid living.

Digital platforms and online communities become pivotal stages for the dance of connection in off-grid living. Through forums, social media groups, and specialized websites, off-grid dwellers find spaces to exchange insights, seek advice, and share their experiences. These virtual connections, often forged across vast geographical distances, become lifelines of support, fostering a sense of belonging in the sometimes solitary journey of off-grid living. The dance of online connection becomes a testament to the adaptability of technology in weaving

practices. The dance of mentorship creates intergenerational bonds, ensuring that the wisdom accumulated over years of off-grid living is preserved and shared within the community.

Challenges in connecting with like-minded individuals in off-grid living include the logistical difficulties of remote locations, adaptability, and considerations for diverse perspectives within the community. The vast distances between off-grid homesteads may pose challenges physically convening as a community, making online platforms essential in fostering connections. The dance of connection requires adaptability, as off-grid living encompasses diverse lifestyles, from wilderness retreats to homesteads on arid plains. Embracing this diversity becomes integral to the dance, encouraging individuals to appreciate the unique challenges and solutions that characterize different off-grid experiences. Additionally, the dance acknowledges the importance of inclusivity, recognizing that off-grid communities are composed of individuals with varied backgrounds, perspectives, and approaches to sustainable living. Building connections requires a mindful dance that respects this diversity and creates spaces for dialogue that transcend individual preferences.

In conclusion, the dance of connecting with like-minded individuals in off-grid living is a dynamic and enriching choreography—a celebration of community that transcends the geographical and ideological boundaries of self-sufficiency. Whether manifested in the virtual realms of online forums or the physical gatherings of homesteading festivals, the dance becomes a testimony to the power of shared values, mutual support, and the collective strength that emerges when individuals come together with a shared vision. In this dance, the heart of off-grid living beats with the rhythms of connection—a harmonious celebration of the bonds that transform the wilderness into a tapestry of shared experiences, resilience, and the enduring spirit of community.

Sharing Resources and Ideas

In the intricate dance of off-grid living, where self-sufficiency meets the rhythms of nature, sharing resources and ideas emerges as a vital and enriching choreography. This communal dance weaves a tapestry of resilience, creativity, and mutual support. The ethos of off-grid living extends beyond individual homesteads, finding expression in the interconnected web of like- minded individuals who recognize the power of collaboration and the collective wisdom that arises when resources and ideas are shared within the community.

At the heart of this dance lies the principle of abundance—

a recognition that the Earth offers a bounty of resources that can be sustainably harnessed and shared among off-grid communities. Shared gardens become lush patches of green, bursting with vegetables, fruits, and herbs extending beyond individual plots' borders. Seeds, the lifeblood of sustainable agriculture, are exchanged among off-grid dwellers, creating a dance of biodiversity that enriches the collective harvest. The dance of shared resources becomes a testament to the abundance of collaboration, where the surplus from one homestead becomes a nourishing gift for another.

The dance of shared ideas unfolds in the digital realms of

online forums, social media groups, and virtual homesteading communities. Off-grid dwellers, often scattered across remote landscapes, leverage these platforms to exchange insights, troubleshoot challenges, and celebrate successes. The dance of shared ideas becomes a dynamic conversation—a collective exploration of sustainable practices, innovative solutions, and time-tested wisdom. Whether discussing rainwater harvesting techniques, off-grid energy systems, or natural building methods, exchanging ideas becomes a lifeline of inspiration that transcends physical distances.

Local gatherings and communal events become stages for the dance of shared resources and ideas to take on tangible forms. Seed swaps, where off-grid gardeners exchange seeds adapted to specific climates, become celebrations of biodiversity and resilience. Skill-sharing workshops become vibrant spaces where individuals teach and learn, passing down traditional crafts, survival skills, and sustainable practices. The dance of shared resources and ideas in these physical gatherings becomes a symphony of diversity, where each participant contributes a unique note to the collective harmony.

In off-grid technology, the dance of shared resources extends to creating open-source solutions. Off-grid communities, recognizing the power of collective innovation, develop and share designs for energy systems, water management tools, and sustainable technologies. The dance becomes a collaborative effort to democratize knowledge, allowing individuals to build upon the shared foundations of off-grid ingenuity. The open-source dance of shared resources empowers off-grid dwellers to co-create a sustainable future, from DIY solar setups to water filtration systems.

Challenges in sharing resources and ideas in off-grid living include the logistics of remote locations, considerations for diverse needs within the community, and the need for mindful communication. The vast distances between off-grid homesteads may pose challenges physically exchanging resources or convening for communal events. In response, digital platforms become essential bridges, facilitating the virtual dance of sharing ideas and resources. The dance also requires an awareness of the diverse needs and preferences within the off-grid community. Recognizing that off-grid living encompasses a spectrum of lifestyles, from minimalist wilderness retreats to permaculture-based homesteads, the dance encourages inclusivity and adaptability. Mindful communication becomes crucial, ensuring that the exchange of resources and ideas is respectful, considerate of individual choices, and fosters a culture of collaboration rather than imposition.

In conclusion, the dance of sharing resources and ideas in off-grid living is a dynamic and symbiotic choreography—a celebration of abundance, ingenuity, and communal support. Whether manifested in the sharing of garden produce, the exchange of seeds, or the collaborative development of open-source technologies, the dance becomes a testimony to the interconnected web that binds off-grid communities. In this dance, the ethos of self-sufficiency harmonizes with the recognition that the true richness of off-grid living lies in the shared wisdom, creativity, and resources that transform the challenges of remote living into opportunities for collective growth. It is a dance that reverberates with the understanding that in the tapestry of shared abundance, the individual threads of each homestead weave together a resilient and thriving community.

Overcoming Social Challenges of Off-Grid Living

In the vast expanse of off-grid living, where the embrace of nature meets the pursuit of self-sufficiency, the social challenges inherent in this lifestyle emerge as a defining frontier. This complex dance requires resilience, adaptability, and a nuanced understanding of human dynamics. As individuals and families venture into the wilderness, seeking solitude and independence, they encounter social challenges that demand intentional efforts to build community, foster connections, and address the potential isolation that can accompany life off the grid.

One of the primary social challenges of off-grid living lies in homesteads' physical remoteness and geographic isolation. In the dance of overcoming this challenge, off-grid communities often leverage digital platforms to establish virtual connections. Online forums, social media groups, and specialized websites become vital stages for off-grid dwellers to share experiences, seek advice, and build a sense of community across vast distances. The dance of virtual connection becomes a lifeline, allowing individuals to transcend geographic isolation and find like- minded companionship in the digital realm. However, it is essential to recognize the limitations of virtual connections and strive for a balance that includes both online and offline interactions to create a comprehensive and robust off-grid community.

Another social challenge stems from the diversity of reasons individuals choose off-grid living, leading to varied lifestyles and approaches. The dance of overcoming this challenge involves fostering inclusivity and respecting the diverse motivations that drive people to embrace this lifestyle. Some may seek solitude for spiritual or philosophical reasons. In contrast, others may be motivated by a desire for environmental stewardship, economic independence, or a return to a more straightforward way of life. Embracing this diversity becomes an integral part of the dance, encouraging a spirit of inclusivity that accommodates different perspectives and lifestyles within the off-grid community.

The pursuit of self-sufficiency can inadvertently lead to isolation, particularly when off-grid dwellers face challenges or require assistance. In the dance of overcoming this challenge, building a culture of mutual support becomes essential. Off-grid communities often develop networks where individuals share knowledge, skills, and resources, creating a safety net that helps navigate the inherent challenges of remote living. The dance of mutual support involves cultivating a mindset that values collaboration and recognizes that every community member brings unique skills and experiences to the collective table. In this dance, the bonds of interdependence replace the potential isolation of self-sufficiency, fostering a spirit of shared resilience.

The social challenge of maintaining community dynamics in off-grid living also includes considerations for conflict resolution and effective communication. The close-knit nature of off-grid communities, where neighbors may be few but interactions are frequent, requires a mindful dance to navigate interpersonal dynamics. Conflict resolution becomes integral to the dance, encouraging open communication, active listening, and a commitment to finding mutually agreeable solutions. Off-grid dwellers often cultivate skills in effective communication, conflict resolution, and emotional intelligence to ensure that community life remains harmonious despite the inevitable challenges that arise.

Children raised in off-grid environments may face unique social challenges, including limited peer access and a different educational experience. In the dance of overcoming these challenges, off-grid families often adopt homeschooling or alternative education approaches to provide a well-rounded education for their children. The challenge becomes an opportunity for creativity and innovation, with off-grid parents crafting educational experiences that align with the principles of their chosen lifestyle. Additionally, intentional efforts are made to foster social interactions for off-grid children, whether through organized community events, online connections with other off-grid families, or visits to nearby towns. Addressing the social challenges for off-grid children involves a holistic approach that considers education and socialization in the unique context of remote living.

Challenges related to maintaining mental health and well-being in off-grid living are another facet of the social dance. The potential isolation, combined with the demands of self-sufficiency, may impact individuals' mental health. Addressing this challenge involves prioritizing mental health, fostering a culture of emotional support within the community, and recognizing when professional help may be necessary. Off-grid communities often emphasize practices that promote well-being, including mindfulness, nature immersion, and intentional social interactions. The dance becomes a collective effort to create an environment where mental health is prioritized, and individuals feel supported in navigating the emotional landscape of off-grid living.

In conclusion, the dance of overcoming social challenges in off-grid living is a nuanced and intentional choreography—a celebration of community building, adaptability, and resilience. Whether addressing physical remoteness, navigating diverse motivations, fostering mutual support, or cultivating effective communication, the dance involves intentional efforts to build connections and create a sense of belonging. In the tapestry of off- grid living, the social dance becomes an integral part of the larger symphony. This harmonious collaboration recognizes the unique challenges of remote living and transforms them into opportunities for communal growth, shared experiences, and a resilient dance of human connection in the wilderness.

CHAPTER X

Financial Planning for Off-Grid Living

Budgeting and Cost Estimates

Embarking on the off-grid journey represents a departure from the conventional rhythms of urban life, introducing a unique set of challenges and opportunities, particularly in finances. The dance of budgeting and cost estimates in off-grid living becomes an intricate choreography, requiring a delicate balance between self-sufficiency and financial prudence. As individuals and families venture into the wilderness, the economic landscape transforms into a dynamic terrain where thoughtful planning, resourcefulness, and a keen understanding of off-grid necessities are paramount.

At the heart of the financial dance lies the art of budgeting—a meticulous process that involves forecasting expenses, allocating resources, and setting financial goals tailored to the demands of off-grid living. The initial steps in this dance often revolve around evaluating the unique needs of the off-grid homestead, encompassing considerations for energy systems, water sources, shelter, and sustenance. The budget becomes a roadmap, guiding off-grid dwellers through the costs of establishing and maintaining an autonomous lifestyle.

Energy systems are a significant pillar in the financial dance of off-grid living. Whether harnessing solar, wind, or hybrid systems, the upfront costs of acquiring and installing renewable energy infrastructure can be substantial. Off-grid dwellers engage in a delicate dance of estimating energy needs, factoring in the variability of renewable sources, and aligning their budgets to achieve energy independence. The dance extends beyond the initial setup to encompass ongoing costs, such as maintenance and potential upgrades, as off-grid individuals seek to balance the upfront investment with the long-term benefits of sustainable and self-generated power.

Water, the essence of life, also commands a prominent role in the financial dance of off-grid living. Establishing reliable water sources through well drilling, rainwater harvesting, or other methods requires careful cost estimation. Off-grid dwellers navigate the dance of water budgeting by considering the availability of local water sources, the climatic conditions influencing rainfall patterns, and the infrastructure needed for water storage and distribution. The ongoing costs involve maintenance, water treatment, and, in some cases, innovations like greywater systems or water recycling initiatives. The dance of water budgeting becomes a crucial aspect of ensuring a consistent and sustainable water supply in remote off-grid locations.

Shelter, often fashioned from natural materials in the spirit of sustainable living, involves both material and labor costs in the financial dance. The budgeting process includes estimates for construction materials, tools, and potentially skilled labor if off-grid dwellers opt for professional assistance. The dance of shelter budgeting also considers ongoing maintenance, repairs, and potential upgrades, recognizing that the resilient structures of off-grid homes require periodic attention in the face of nature's elements.

The sustenance aspect of the off-grid dance involves budgeting for food production, preservation, and occasional supplementary purchases. Off-grid dwellers cultivate gardens, tend to livestock, and adopt sustainable agricultural practices to minimize reliance on external food sources. The budgeting dance extends to considerations for seeds, fertilizers, livestock care, and equipment for food preservation techniques such as canning or dehydrating. While the goal is often self-sufficiency in food production, the dance acknowledges the fabric of the community, allowing individuals to transcend physical isolation and build bonds that resonate with the ethos of self-sufficiency.

Local gatherings and off-grid events emerge as vibrant episodes in the dance of community building. Off-grid expos, homesteading festivals, and skill-sharing workshops allow like-minded individuals to converge, exchange ideas, and foster community. In these gatherings, the dance takes on a tangible and embodied form, with individuals sharing practical skills, showcasing sustainable practices, and strengthening the ties that bind them in their pursuit of off-grid living. The dance of physical connection becomes a celebration of diversity within the off-grid community—recognizing that each individual brings a unique set of skills, experiences, and perspectives to the collective table.

The dance of connecting with like-minded individuals extends beyond shared ideals of self-sufficiency to encompass broader themes of sustainability, ecological stewardship, and reverence for the natural world. Off-grid communities often find themselves at the forefront of environmental consciousness, and the connections forged within these circles become conduits for exchanging eco-friendly practices. The dance becomes an opportunity to learn about innovative off-grid technologies, sustainable agriculture techniques, and conservation efforts that align with the principles of stewardship. The off-grid community is connected through the sustainability dance, forming a network of people dedicated to living sustainably.

In the dance of connection, mentorship emerges as a guiding force, passing wisdom from seasoned off-grid veterans to those embarking on the journey. The exchange of practical knowledge, survival skills, and time-tested strategies becomes a cherished aspect of community building. Mentors become beacons of support, offering insights on everything from renewable energy systems and water conservation to sustainable building the need for flexibility and occasional adjustments, especially in the early stages of establishing productive gardens or integrating livestock into off-grid life.

The financial dance of off-grid living incorporates considerations for waste management, with budgeting extending to composting systems, recycling initiatives, and potential waste-to-energy solutions. The upfront costs of implementing efficient waste management practices are weighed against the long-term benefits of minimizing environmental impact and promoting sustainability. The dance involves the financial aspects and the integration of waste management practices into the broader ethos of off-grid living, where resourcefulness and conservation take center stage.

Challenges in the budgeting dance of off-grid living include the potential for unexpected costs, adaptability, and ongoing financial sustainability considerations. Off-grid dwellers recognize the inherent unpredictability of remote living, where unforeseen challenges such as equipment breakdowns, extreme weather events, or changes in regulatory requirements can impact budgets. The dance entails saving money for emergencies, encouraging flexibility to deal with unanticipated situations, and embracing an inventive mentality to solve problems in an environmentally friendly way. Ongoing economic sustainability becomes a focal point, with the dance evolving as off-grid dwellers refine their budgeting strategies based on lessons learned, changing circumstances, and advancements in off-grid technologies.

Cost estimates in the dance of off-grid living also extend to land acquisition or lease considerations, legal requirements, and potential permits. The financial landscape encompasses the tangible costs of infrastructure and sustenance and the legal and regulatory aspects of establishing an off-grid homestead. Off-grid dwellers meticulously research local regulations, understand zoning requirements, and estimate the costs associated with legal compliance. The dance of legal and regulatory considerations becomes integral to the financial choreography, ensuring that off-grid living aligns with legal frameworks while minimizing potential financial setbacks.

In the dance of off-grid finances, the delicate interplay between self-sufficiency and financial prudence becomes a key theme. Off-grid dwellers seek to meet their basic needs autonomously and do so in a way that aligns with their financial goals and values. The dance involves continuous learning, adaptation, and a willingness to embrace the evolving landscape of off-grid living. As the economic dance unfolds, off-grid dwellers find themselves navigating the challenges and discovering the rich tapestry of possibilities that arise when financial stewardship harmonizes with the principles of self-sufficiency and sustainable living. In this intricate dance, the wilderness becomes a stage for resilience, resourcefulness, and the enduring pursuit of financial independence in the heart of nature.

Income Generation Off the Grid

In the dance of off-grid living, where the cadence of nature harmonizes with the pursuit of self-sufficiency, income generation emerges as a crucial melody in the overall symphony. The unique lifestyle of off-grid dwellers, often characterized by remote locations and a commitment to sustainability, prompts a thoughtful choreography of income-generating activities. The narrative of financial independence and self-sustainable livelihoods takes center stage as individuals and families navigate the intricate dance of earning a living while treading lightly on the Earth.

One of the primary considerations in the dance of income generation off the grid is embracing alternative employment models that resonate with the principles of sustainable living. Remote work and freelancing have become viable options for off-grid dwellers, facilitated by advancements in technology that connect individuals to a global job market without being tethered to urban centers. The dance involves the exploration of online platforms, where skills ranging from graphic design to programming can be leveraged to secure income. The flexibility of remote work aligns seamlessly with the off- grid lifestyle, allowing individuals to earn a living while enjoying the tranquility of their natural surroundings.

Entrepreneurship emerges as a critical player in the income generation dance-off-the-grid, with off-grid dwellers harnessing their skills and creativity to establish small businesses. From artisanal crafts and handmade products to specialized services such as eco-tourism or permaculture consulting, the entrepreneurial dance celebrates individual passions converging with economic viability. The spirit of self-sufficiency extends to the creation of marketable goods and services that contribute to financial stability and reflect the values and ethos of off-grid living.

The fertile grounds of off-grid homesteads often lead to the cultivation of sustainable and locally focused enterprises. The dance of income generation involves tapping into the land's agricultural potential, with organic farming, permaculture, and agroforestry practices becoming viable avenues for livelihoods. The sale of fresh produce, artisanal goods, or value-added products such as jams and preserves amplifies the income potential while fostering a connection between off-grid dwellers and their local communities. In this dance, the land becomes a source of sustenance and a foundation for economic resilience.

Tourism, when approached sustainably, becomes another note in the income generation melody. Off-grid locations, with their pristine natural beauty and unique lifestyle, often attract those seeking eco-friendly and immersive experiences. The dance of income generation involves creating sustainable tourism ventures, whether through eco-retreats, guided nature tours, or educational workshops. Off-grid dwellers become stewards of their environments, sharing their knowledge and way of life with visitors while generating income that supports their livelihoods.

The dance of income generation off the grid extends beyond tangible goods and services to embrace the digital realm. Content creation, blogging, and social media become avenues for off-grid dwellers to share their experiences, skills, and insights, creating additional income streams. When woven into engaging and educational content, the narrative of off-grid living resonates with a global audience interested in sustainable lifestyles, further expanding the economic possibilities for those living off the grid.

The traditional skills honed in off-grid living, from carpentry and blacksmithing to herbalism and natural building, find a market in the dance of income generation. Off-grid dwellers, often equipped with a diverse skill set born out of necessity, can offer workshops, online courses, or consultancy services to those seeking to learn traditional and sustainable practices. The transfer of skills becomes a source of income and a means of preserving and sharing the wisdom embedded in off-grid living.

Challenges in the dance of income generation off the grid include navigating the digital divide, adapting to market demands, and addressing the seasonality of certain activities. While remote work and online entrepreneurship offer vast opportunities, off-grid dwellers may face challenges related to internet connectivity and access to digital platforms. The dance involves finding creative solutions, such as satellite internet or community-based initiatives, to bridge the digital gap and ensure a reliable online presence.

Adapting to market demands becomes an ongoing theme in income generation. Off-grid entrepreneurs must stay attuned to consumer preferences, trends, and emerging opportunities to ensure the relevance and success of their ventures. The dance involves a continuous learning process, with off-grid dwellers honing their business acumen and adapting their offerings to align with the dynamic landscape of market demands.

The seasonality of certain income-generating activities, particularly agriculture or tourism-related ones, poses another challenge in the dance off the grid. Off-grid dwellers navigate the rhythm of nature, understanding that certain ventures may be more viable during specific seasons. The dance entails planning for seasonal variations, diversifying sources of income, and adopting an all-encompassing strategy that considers the cyclical nature of off-grid living.

In conclusion, the dance of income generation off the grid is a multifaceted and dynamic choreography—a celebration of resilience, creativity, and the fusion of sustainable practices with economic viability. Whether through remote work, entrepreneurship, sustainable agriculture, or tourism, off-grid dwellers engage in a harmonious dance that supports their livelihoods and contributes to the broader narrative of sustainable and self-sufficient living. In this dance, the wilderness becomes a stage for economic ingenuity, where the pursuit of financial independence intertwines with the rhythms of nature, creating a melody that echoes the transformative possibilities of income generation off the grid.

Long-Term Financial Sustainability

In the intricate dance of off-grid living, where self-sufficiency and sustainability take center stage, pursuing long-term financial sustainability becomes a strategic and essential choreography. The unique lifestyle of off-grid dwellers, often characterized by remote locations and a commitment to harmonizing with nature, demands a thoughtful and forward-looking approach to financial planning. As individuals and families embrace the challenge of living off the grid, they embark on a journey that involves navigating the complexities of income generation, resource management, and resilience against unforeseen obstacles to ensure a sustainable financial future.

Central to the dance of long-term financial sustainability is the establishment of diversified income streams. Off-grid dwellers recognize the inherent volatility of specific income sources, such as seasonal agricultural endeavors or tourism-related activities. The dance involves creating a financial portfolio encompassing multiple avenues, from remote work and entrepreneurship to sustainable agriculture and local services. Diversification protects against the unpredictable, allowing off-grid individuals to weather fluctuations in specific sectors while maintaining a steady overall income.

Investing in renewable energy infrastructure emerges as a critical note in the dance of long-term financial sustainability. Off-grid dwellers often invest upfront in solar panels, wind turbines, or other sustainable energy systems to achieve autonomy and reduce ongoing energy costs. The dance extends beyond the initial setup to include considerations for regular maintenance, potential upgrades, and the integration of energy-efficient technologies. Investing in renewable energy becomes a cornerstone for financial savings over time and aligns with the ethos of environmental stewardship.

Resourcefulness takes center stage in the dance of long-term financial sustainability, with off-grid dwellers embracing repurposing and upcycling to extend the lifespan of materials and equipment. The dance involves finding innovative solutions to repair, reuse, and refurbish items, minimizing the need for frequent replacements and reducing overall expenses. The ethos of resourcefulness contributes to financial sustainability and aligns with the waste reduction and conservation principles that define off-grid living.

Water management becomes a pivotal theme in the dance of financial sustainability, with off-grid dwellers investing in systems for rainwater harvesting, efficient water use, and recycling. The upfront costs of establishing reliable water sources and sustainable water management practices contribute to long-term financial stability by reducing reliance on external water supplies and minimizing ongoing expenses. The dance involves meticulously considering water needs, local climatic conditions, and infrastructure investments that pay dividends over time.

In the quest for long-term financial sustainability, off-grid dwellers often embrace a minimalist lifestyle, focusing on needs rather than wants. The dance involves conscious choices in consumption, prioritizing quality over quantity and favoring durable, energy-efficient items aligned with sustainable practices. By adopting a minimalist mindset, off-grid individuals reduce their ecological footprint and enhance financial resilience, freeing resources for essential needs and long-term investments.

Emergency preparedness is a fundamental posture in the dance of long-term financial sustainability. Off-grid dwellers recognize the potential for unexpected challenges, whether natural disasters, equipment failures, or economic downturns. The dance entails building financial safety nets, reserving funds for emergencies, and formulating plans for handling unanticipated events. Emergency preparedness becomes a cornerstone of financial sustainability, offering a safety net that empowers off-grid individuals to face challenges with resilience and adaptability.

Managing the long-term expenses of infrastructure and maintenance, addressing the possible impact of other economic forces, and striking a balance between self-sufficiency and external dependencies are some challenges in long-term financial sustainability. While the goal of self-sufficiency is paramount in off-grid living, a delicate dance exists in recognizing when external support, such as community collaboration or shared resources, can enhance financial stability without compromising independence. The dance involves finding the right balance that aligns with individual values and long-term goals.

External economic factors, including inflation, market trends, and global economic shifts, may impact the long-term financial sustainability of off-grid living. The dance involves staying informed about economic dynamics, adapting income-generating activities to market demands, and making strategic adjustments to financial plans in response to changing conditions. The ability to pivot and adjust becomes a crucial skill in the dance, ensuring that long-term financial sustainability remains resilient despite external economic influences.

Managing the long-term costs associated with infrastructure and maintenance requires a nuanced approach to financial sustainability. Off-grid dwellers must carefully weigh the upfront investment against the ongoing benefits and savings derived from sustainable practices and infrastructure. The dance involves adopting a lifecycle perspective, considering the durability and efficiency of materials and systems to optimize long-term financial outcomes. Regular maintenance, proactive upgrades, and a commitment to efficient resource use contribute to the enduring economic sustainability of off-grid living.

In conclusion, the dance of long-term financial sustainability in off-grid living is a nuanced and intentional choreography—a celebration of diversification, resourcefulness, and resilience. Whether through diversified income streams, investments in renewable energy, or conscious choices in consumption, off-grid dwellers engage in a harmonious dance that supports their current lifestyle and lays the foundation for a prosperous and sustainable financial future. In this dance, the wilderness becomes a backdrop for economic ingenuity, where the pursuit of long-term financial stability intertwines with the rhythms of nature, creating a melody that echoes the transformative possibilities of financial sustainability off the grid.

CHAPTER XI

Overcoming Common Off-Grid Challenges

Dealing with Isolation

In the vast expanses of off-grid living, where the echoes of nature reverberate and self-sufficiency is a guiding ethos, the challenge of isolation emerges as a poignant note in the symphony of this unconventional lifestyle. Off- grid dwellers, drawn to remote landscapes for their tranquility and independence, must confront the complex dance of dealing with isolation. This dance requires resilience, intentionality, and a nuanced understanding of the mental and emotional landscapes that unfold in solitude.

Isolation in off-grid living is a multifaceted experience, encompassing physical remoteness from urban centers, limited access to community amenities, and the potential absence of nearby neighbors. The dance involves reconciling the desire for solitude with the need for social connection as off-grid dwellers navigate the balance between the self-sufficiency that drew them to remote locations and the innate human need for companionship.

One aspect of the dance involves leveraging digital technologies to bridge the physical gaps that isolation can create. Off-grid dwellers embrace the virtual realm, using the internet to connect with like-minded individuals, participate in online communities, and maintain ties with friends and family. The dance of dealing with isolation becomes a harmonious integration of technology into the off-grid lifestyle, fostering a sense of connectedness that transcends physical distances.

Community-building takes center stage in the dance of dealing with isolation. Off-grid dwellers recognize the importance of cultivating a local support network through intentional community living or regular gatherings with nearby neighbors. The dance involves creating opportunities for shared experiences, skill-sharing, and mutual support, fostering a sense of camaraderie that transforms physical remoteness into a backdrop for meaningful connections.

Engaging in intentional activities becomes a crucial note in dealing with isolation. Off-grid dwellers often immerse themselves in the natural beauty surrounding them, embracing outdoor pursuits, creative endeavors, and mindfulness practices that fill their time and contribute to a sense of purpose and fulfillment. The dance involves finding joy and meaning in solitary moments, transforming isolation into an opportunity for self-discovery and personal growth.

Self-sufficiency becomes a guiding principle in dealing with isolation, empowering off-grid dwellers to meet their needs and cultivate independence. The dance involves acquiring essential skills, from food production and water management to basic DIY repairs, creating a foundation for self-reliance that minimizes the potential challenges of isolation. The ethos of self-sufficiency transforms isolation into a chosen path rather than an imposition, allowing off-grid dwellers to navigate solitude with confidence and resilience.

Challenges in dealing with isolation include the potential for loneliness, adaptability, and mental and emotional well-being considerations. While solitude is often a deliberate choice in off-grid living, the potential for loneliness remains a natural and human experience. The dance involves recognizing and addressing feelings of isolation through digital connections, community engagement, or introspective practices that foster a sense of inner fulfillment.

Adaptability becomes a recurring theme in the dance of dealing with isolation. Off-grid dwellers must navigate the ebb and flow of seasons, weather patterns, and potential challenges in remote locations. The dance involves a flexible mindset, embracing change, and finding creative solutions to overcome obstacles that may amplify the sense of isolation. Adaptability becomes essential in transforming isolation into an ever-evolving landscape of opportunities.

Mental and emotional well-being stand as foundational elements in the dance of dealing with isolation. Off-grid dwellers prioritize practices that promote mindfulness, resilience, and a positive mindset. The dance entails spending time in nature, participating in joyful activities, and recognizing when further help might be required. Mental health becomes a focal point in the overall well-being of off-grid individuals, allowing them to navigate isolation with a sense of equilibrium and emotional strength.

In conclusion, the dance of dealing with isolation in off-grid living is a nuanced and intentional choreography—a celebration of connectedness, self-sufficiency, and adaptability. Whether through digital connections, community-building, planned activities, or a commitment to mental well-being, off-grid dwellers engage in a harmonious dance that mitigates the challenges of isolation and transforms solitude into a canvas for personal fulfillment and growth. In this dance, the wilderness becomes a sanctuary for self-discovery, where the rhythms of nature harmonize with the intricate steps of navigating isolation in the pursuit of an unconventional and fulfilling off-grid lifestyle.

Managing Limited Resources

In the tapestry of off-grid living, where the rhythm of nature dictates the pace, managing limited resources is a defining choreography. Off-grid dwellers, drawn to remote landscapes for the promise of self-sufficiency and a harmonious relationship with the environment, embark on a dance that requires astute planning, resourcefulness, and a deep appreciation for the finite nature of the resources at their disposal. Managing limited resources in off-grid living becomes an intricate art, weaving together sustainability, resilience, and a profound understanding of the delicate balance between human needs and the natural world's capacity.

Water, the elixir of life, emerges as a central theme in managing limited resources. Off-grid dwellers navigate the challenge of water scarcity by adopting practices such as rainwater harvesting, efficient water use, and recycling. The dance entails estimating water requirements, accounting for regional climate variations, and making infrastructure investments that optimize water efficiency. By embracing the art of water management, off-grid individuals ensure a reliable water supply and contribute to preserving this precious resource in their natural surroundings.

Energy, harnessed from renewable sources, becomes another note in the symphony of resource management. Off-grid dwellers embrace solar panels, wind turbines, and other sustainable technologies to generate power harmoniously with the environment. The dance involves strategic planning to optimize energy production, storage, and distribution, recognizing the intermittent nature of renewable sources. By managing limited energy resources effectively, off-grid individuals not only meet their needs autonomously but also reduce their ecological footprint, creating a dance that harmonizes with the rhythms of nature.

Cultivating food, often intertwined with the natural landscape, becomes a dynamic partner in resource management. Off-grid dwellers engage in sustainable agriculture, permaculture, and agroforestry practices to maximize the yield from limited land. The dance involves soil conservation, companion planting, and water-efficient irrigation methods. By nurturing the land and practicing regenerative agriculture, off-grid individuals secure their food supply and contribute to the health and resilience of the ecosystems supporting their lifestyle.

Waste, viewed as a potential resource, takes center stage in the dance of resource management. Off-grid dwellers adopt composting, recycling, and upcycling practices to minimize waste and repurpose materials. The dance incorporates making thoughtful consumption decisions, lowering dependency on single-use goods, and ingeniously turning trash into valuable resources. By managing limited resources with a waste-conscious mindset, off-grid individuals contribute to a healthier environment and embrace a sustainable lifestyle that aligns with conservation principles.

Time, recognized as a valuable and finite resource, becomes a focal point in the dance of off-grid living. Off-grid dwellers prioritize tasks, plan for seasonal variations, and embrace a slower pace that aligns with the natural rhythms of their surroundings. The dance involves intentionally allocating time for essential activities, from food production and maintenance to community engagement and personal well-being. By managing time effectively, off-grid individuals create a harmonious dance that balances productivity with a deep connection to the natural world.

Challenges in managing limited resources include the potential for unpredictability, the need for adaptability, and considerations for ongoing maintenance. Off-grid dwellers recognize the inherent unpredictability of remote living, where factors such as weather events, equipment breakdowns, or changes in natural patterns may impact resource availability. The dance fosters adaptability, develops contingency plans, and embraces a mindset that navigates unforeseen challenges with resilience and creativity.

Ongoing infrastructure and systems maintenance becomes a recurring theme in the dance of resource management. Off-grid dwellers must balance the initial investments in renewable energy, water systems, and agricultural practices with the long-term costs associated with maintenance and potential upgrades. The dance involves strategic planning to ensure the enduring viability of essential systems, recognizing that regular attention and care are integral to the sustainability of off- grid living.

In conclusion, the dance of managing limited resources in off-grid living is a nuanced and intentional choreography—a celebration of sustainability, resilience, and the delicate interplay between human needs and the capacity of the natural world. Whether through water management, energy efficiency, regenerative agriculture, waste-conscious practices, or the intentional allocation of time, off-grid dwellers engage in a harmonious dance that meets their needs and contributes to the well-being of the ecosystems supporting their chosen lifestyle. In this dance, the wilderness becomes a stage for resourceful ingenuity, where the pursuit of self-sufficiency harmonizes with the intricate steps of managing limited resources in the dance of off-grid living.

Staying Safe and Healthy

In the rugged embrace of off-grid living, where the natural world sets the stage, and self-sufficiency is a guiding principle, the pursuit of staying safe and healthy becomes a nuanced and integral dance. Off-grid dwellers, drawn to remote landscapes for the promise of autonomy and a closer connection to nature, engage in a choreography that goes beyond mere survival—it is a celebration of holistic well-being. The dance involves a delicate interplay between physical health, mental resilience, and a deep understanding of the environmental factors shaping the off-grid experience.

Physical health takes center stage in the dance of staying safe and healthy. Off-grid dwellers recognize the importance of a well-rounded and nutritious diet, often sourced from their gardens and local resources. The dance involves cultivating sustainable food practices, from organic farming to permaculture, ensuring a diverse and nutrient-rich diet that supports overall health. Regular physical activity becomes a natural part of the dance through outdoor pursuits, homesteading tasks, or intentional exercise routines that align with the off-grid lifestyle.

Water, the lifeblood of well-being, becomes a pivotal theme in staying safe and healthy. Off-grid dwellers manage carefully, from sourcing clean water through methods like rainwater harvesting to adopting efficient water use practices. The dance involves maintaining water quality through filtration and purification methods, recognizing that access to safe drinking water is fundamental to health in remote locations. Integrating water-conscious practices becomes a harmonious step in the overall choreography of well-being.

Mental resilience and emotional well-being are crucial in staying safe and healthy off-grid living. The tranquility of nature and the autonomy of self-sufficiency contribute to a unique psychological landscape. Still, off-grid dwellers also navigate potential challenges such as isolation and the unpredictability of remote living. The dance involves embracing mindfulness practices, fostering a positive mindset, and recognizing mental health's importance in the overall well-being journey. Community engagement, both local and virtual, becomes a supportive note in the dance, providing connections that contribute to emotional resilience.

In the dance of staying safe and healthy, shelter and living arrangements become integral considerations. Off- grid dwellers craft homes from natural materials, embracing sustainable building practices prioritizing health and environmental impact. The dance involves ensuring proper ventilation, insulation, and waste management to create living spaces that promote well- being. The intentional design of homes aligns with principles of comfort, energy efficiency, and harmony with the natural surroundings, creating a holistic approach to shelter that supports overall health.

Healthcare in off-grid living takes on a proactive and preventive character. The dance involves cultivating herbal gardens for natural remedies, embracing traditional healing practices, and acquiring skills in first aid. Off-grid dwellers often develop a deeper connection to their local ecosystems, tapping into the medicinal properties of native plants. The dance of healthcare extends beyond immediate needs to include a holistic approach that integrates natural remedies, preventive measures, and a keen awareness of the body's symbiotic relationship with the environment.

Challenges in staying safe and healthy include the potential for emergencies, the need for adaptability, and considerations for accessing medical care. Off-grid dwellers recognize the importance of emergency preparedness, engaging in the dance of learning first aid, acquiring survival skills, and developing contingency plans for unforeseen circumstances. The dance involves fostering adaptability, embracing a mindset that navigates challenges with resilience, and finding creative solutions when immediate access to medical care may be limited.

Access to medical care is critical to staying safe and healthy off-grid living. While off-grid dwellers often adopt a self-sufficient mindset, the dance involves recognizing when professional medical intervention is necessary. The remote nature of off-grid locations may pose challenges in accessing healthcare facilities, making the dance a delicate balance between self-sufficiency and knowing when to seek external support. Telemedicine and collaborative community initiatives become potential partners in the dance, enhancing access to medical advice and resources.

In conclusion, the dance of staying safe and healthy in off-grid living is a holistic and intentional choreography—a celebration of physical vitality, mental resilience, and a harmonious relationship with the natural environment. Whether through sustainable food practices, water management, mental well-being strategies, shelter design, or proactive healthcare measures, off-grid dwellers engage in a harmonious dance that safeguards their health and fosters a deep connection to the rhythms of nature. In this dance, the wilderness becomes a canvas for well-being, where the pursuit of staying safe and healthy intertwines with the intricate steps of off-grid living.

CONCLUSION

In the closing act of "Eco Endeavors: A Handbook of Off-Grid Projects - Crafting a Greener, Smarter, and Independent Lifestyle," the essence of the off-grid journey comes to fruition. This comprehensive guide has taken readers on a transformative odyssey, exploring the multifaceted realms of sustainable living, self-sufficiency, and harmonious coexistence with the natural world.

As the final curtain descends, the resounding message is clear: the off-grid lifestyle is not merely a collection of projects but a profound philosophy, a commitment to crafting a life that reverberates with eco-conscious choices and intentional living. The handbook's chapters, each a choreographed step in the dance of off-grid living, have unveiled the intricacies of essential skills, resource management, and the cultivation of holistic well-being.

The echo of the handbook's title, "Eco Endeavors," encapsulates the spirit of the off-grid journey—a ceaseless pursuit of endeavors prioritizing ecological harmony. It goes beyond the conventional notions of sustainability, delving into a realm where every decision is made to minimize environmental impact and forge a path toward a regenerative and more intelligent lifestyle.

Crafting a greener, more intelligent, and independent lifestyle is not a static achievement. Still, it is an ongoing dance that adapts to nature's rhythms, embraces innovation, and fosters a deep connection to the Earth. The handbook, with its diverse array of projects and insights, serves not as a rigid roadmap but a compass, guiding individuals toward a more intentional and fulfilling existence.

In the final pages, readers are invited to carry the torch of Eco Endeavors forward, weaving knowledge and practices into the fabric of their lives. As illuminated by this handbook, the off-grid lifestyle is not an isolated choice but a community-driven, global movement. It is a testament to the power of collective action in shaping a future where individuals, empowered by the wisdom shared in these pages, can forge a sustainable path toward a greener, more intelligent, and more independent world. As the curtain falls on this handbook, the stage is set for a new chapter in the dance of Eco Endeavors. In this choreography, every reader becomes active, contributing to the ongoing narrative of a regenerative and harmonious way of life.

Thank you for buying and reading/listening to our book. If you found this book useful/helpful please take a few minutes and leave a review on the platform where you purchased our book. Your feedback matters greatly to us.